# Embedding Subversion and Gender Identity

## 'Ulti', the Secret Language of the Hijra-Koti Community

# Embedding Subversion and Gender Identity

## 'Ulti', the Secret Language of the Hijra-Koti Community

ENAKSHI NANDI

Tulika Books

Published by

**Tulika Books**
44 (first floor), Shahpur Jat, New Delhi 110 049, India
www.tulikabooks.in



First edition (hardback) 2024

ISBN: 978-81-956392-5-0

Printed at Chaman Offset, Delhi 110 002

*to the hijra and koti community*
*and the secrets whispered*
*in subversive silences*

# Contents

# Foreword

The study of language is simultaneously the study of the human mind as well as of how human subjectivities shape, and are shaped by, human societies. Linguistics as a discipline proposes to study both these aspects of an individual (and the collectives they participate in), but in practice this usually entails cleavages in focus: very often, studies of individual languages examine *either* the formal properties of a language (such as its morphology, syntax, phonology, etc) *or* the sociology of its speakers, their attitudes towards using it, and the discursive and social meanings that arise. Only extremely rarely are the dual preoccupations of linguistics necessarily synthesized to provide a complete account of both the form and the use of a language. Enakshi Nandi's study of Ulti, a language spoken by the hijra-koti community in West Bengal, is therefore already unusual, as it argues ably that if we are to understand the shape of words and aspects of the grammar of Ulti, we need to adopt a holistic approach to what a language is, both in society as well as in the minds of its speakers.

Nandi's study of Ulti is significant because it argues that many aspects of Ulti must be sourced to the hijra-koti community's sociocultural, economic, political and occupational marginalization in contemporary (and historical) cisnormative and heteropatriarchal society. The language is a 'secret' language spoken only within the hijra-koti community, and it serves as both a place of self-expression and refuge. Its lexical items and grammatical rules, Nandi argues, also perform this dual function – Ulti enables its woman-identifying transgender speakers to performatively present (aspects of) gender identity and to mark their identification with the community at large, as well as to mask the content of their speech from a discriminatory and often perilously violent world. Importantly, rather than merely asserting the social role that Ulti plays for its speakers, Nandi demonstrates to us how aspects of the linguistic structure of Ulti words and sentences conspire to effect the dual role that the language plays in its speakers' lives. For example, the important linguistic strategy of 'feminization' of nouns that Nandi describes simultaneously indexes the distinctness of the speaker's gender ascription, and encrypts the referent of the noun phase in such a way that it becomes inaccessible to the non-Ulti speaker. As Nandi argues, this 'symbolic gender' marker does not however yield a grammatically relevant gender feature that ends up shown as verb agreement on the verb, or change the features of the noun/noun phrase in a way that demands anything other than the syntax of Bangla. Through this creation of a grammatical category which systematically functions as a kind of palimpsest on the grammatical system of Bangla, Ulti speakers create a medium in which the self can be expressed.

Nandi shows us that Ulti speakers' conscious manipulation of certain aspects of lexis, rules of word and sentence formation does not displace Bangla, and argues that it is best analysed as a register of Bangla. In my opinion, this raises very interesting questions for the ways linguists perceive language. For example, it would not be unreasonable to say that Ulti is not an 'I-language' in Chomsky's sense: it is not the psychological property of an individual or an externalization of a knowledge state of the mind – the extra features (in terms of lexical items and system morphemes) do not signal a departure from the knowledge state which yields us Bangla. Since it is nobody's first language, and is acquired by a process that is entirely based on exposure to the community, it could be said that Ulti is best characterized as an E-language, and therefore only of peripheral interest to linguistic theory.

However, Ulti resists such an easy dismissal from its claims to relevance. For one, Nandi shows us that Ulti is describable as a language *system*, which is amenable to the same sort of context-sensitivity and mixing as regular I-languages are. Is this an indicator of the strength of analogical reasoning that having an innate language ability endows us with, and which arguably underlies human ability to construct languages for humour and other aesthetic pleasure? Are there differences between consciously constructed languages and languages like Ulti? To complicate matters, take also on board Nandi's observation that Ulti has begun to develop grammatical elements and processes distinct from Bangla ones, and that we are most likely witnessing an early stage of the development of an independent language. Whether Ulti will go the full way to an independent language or not, as Nandi herself points out, is not within the realm of a linguist's prediction, but these minimal innovations already pose interesting questions for linguistic theory – can at least some E-languages transition to become I-language states, given the correct social circumstances, and therefore begin to see intergenerational transmission? Watching languages like Ulti is essential, and Nandi's fine-grained discussion of its word and sentence structure sets the base for future work.

Ulti is also important for expanding our understanding of the question of language and identity, key topics in sociolinguistics and the social sciences. Much of the current debate worldwide rests on perspectives that are informed by languages that index gender identity and sexual preference by either gendered pronouns or verb agreement, both of which are absent in the language which forms the spine of Ulti, Bangla. The importance of this ground-breaking study of Ulti lies not only in the specific morphological strategies it has made in representing the self of the transgender Bangla-Ulti speaker, it also underscores the crucial importance of linguistic analysis in a truly diverse and inclusive discussion.

To end on a personal note, I am delighted to see this book appear in print a (relatively) short while after a version of this manuscript was defended as a PhD at Jawaharlal Nehru University. As I write these last few words, I think back to the beginning of Enakshi's journey when she first articulated her decision to work with the hijra-koti community on their language. Our intention then was quite a simple one: we were going to study Ulti from the usual framework that linguists working on minor languages employ, that is, describe the grammar, study the attitudes that speakers had to it and the world had to its speakers, and hope that this piece of research will build prestige for the language and encourage speakers to keep it alive as a crucial marker of their identity. What we encountered instead was a language that did not need our efforts at preservation, speakers who spoke it to assert their very distinct selves, and were eager to share with Enakshi a seat at their window into the world and their minds, subverting, in the process, many of the certainties that linguists like us have embedded in our minds. I can only thank Enakshi for taking me along on this wondrous, and deeply educative, journey, which is now yours to enjoy!

*January 2024* AYESHA KIDWAI

the invigilator, who enquired whether Hema had changed her gender anywhere else, which she denied. The invigilator then took the matter to the SSC Board (Staff Selection Commission Board) which was conducting the exam. Hema describes her interaction with the invigilator and the Board members in the excerpt below, where 'H' refers to Hema and 'E' refers to this author.

Excerpt 1

H: *Akta lok esche, eshe bolche, 'Ki hoyeche?' Ami bolchi amar admit ta 'female' e esche, amar sob documents 'male' e. Bolche, 'accha dekhi.' Tarpor amar jeta ami application korechilam se application form ta dekhalam, to application number diye dekhlo sob. Ami 'male' e form ta fill up korechilam. To bhul ta oderi, orai pathiyeche eta 'female' e kore. To ami bollam, 'Amar photo ta dekhe hoyto 'female' koreche, seta to oder bhul.* ***Amar photo dekhei ba keno amake chinhito korbe?*** *Amar to gender ami likhe diyechilam oikhantate. Bolche,* ***'Tumi ki lekho?'*** *Khub sundor bhabei je . . . ami ki likhi . . . jehetu amake dekhe se to bujhte parchena . . .* ***ami abar bolchi ami male, aar odike esche female, ami dekhte ar ek ajooba*** *. . . bolche 'tumi ki lekho?'*
E: *Ajooba na . . .*
H: *Ora setai mone korche. Puro hall tar moddhe 32 jon boshe, tar moddhe ami eka erokom. Bolche 'tumi ki lekho nije?' Ami bolchi, 'ami "male" likhi.'*

Translation

H: One [from the SSC] person came and asked 'What happened?' I said, 'My admit [card] says [I'm] "female", all my documents list "male".' They said, 'Let's see it.' I showed them my application form, which they checked against my application number. I had filled up my form as 'male'. So the mistake was theirs; they sent the admit card reading 'female'. So I said, 'Perhaps they saw my photograph and labelled me "female", but that is their fault. **Why should anyone label me "female" just by looking at my photo?** I had clearly specified my gender in there.' They asked me, **'What do you write?'** . . . very nicely . . . what do I write . . . because they couldn't understand just by looking at me. **I'm saying I'm male, the card says 'female', I look like another *ajooba*** [strange being – referring to her androgynous/femme appearance lent by a kurti and palazzo suit and long hair]. . . . They asked, 'What do you write?'
E: Not an *ajooba* . . .
H: That's what they must have been thinking. Out of the thirty-two people in the hall, I was the only one like this. They asked, 'What do you write as your gender?' I said, 'I write "male".' (Interview with Hema)

The issue was soon resolved without much hassle: Hema was advised to sit for the exam and take up the matter with the Board later, who were responsible for the *faux pas* in the first place. The sensitivity and respect shown by the authority figures to Hema when they asked her how she writes her name (instead of the typical callous questions anticipated in such situations, like 'What are you?') made a deep impression on Hema, who was amazed and delighted at the way the question was phrased – respectful of her subjectivity and focusing on her agency in choosing her gender.

This experience influenced her comment on their perceptible confusion regarding her ambiguous gender identity, which was tonally indulgent even as it was critical of their instinct to see a person's name, appearance, presentation and gender identity align with conventional binary categories of gender. She was however significantly less impressed by whoever had printed the 'wrong' gender on her admit card, and questioned their reductive and essentialized gender assumptions and the need to 'correct' her gender to what they thought was the right one for a transwoman, even though she had already filled 'male' in her application form and despite the masculine name on the admit card – 'Why should anyone label me "female" just by looking at my photo?' she quipped. It did not matter that they probably intended to be trans-friendly; what rankled was their inability or refusal to acknowledge the complexity and multiplicity of the koti subjectivity and accept Hema's choice of gender in her form.

This anecdote prompted me to dig deeper into her reasons for not changing her gender in her official documents, when she does not shy away from embracing her femininity and transgender identity in her personal, professional and social life. Her responses were revealing. Her first reason was that she was 'comfortable' identifying as 'male' in her official documents because she is biologically male; further, 'why should I identify as a woman when I'm not one and claim one of the seats reserved for women in government jobs?'

Her second reason had to do with retaining her personal freedom of mobility and access. Many countries do not officially recognize 'transgender' as a gender identity, so persons whose passports list them as such face problems at airport immigration in those countries. Hema recounted an incident where a group of transgenders from India went for a conference to Amsterdam. Despite being similarly attired in femme/feminine clothing, those among them whose passports said 'male' were let through, while those whose passports said 'transgender' were held back. It was a while before the officials found a way to resolve the matter and allowed them into the country.

Her third reason simply had to do with not wanting to deal with the bureaucratic tedium and harassment of getting one's personal details changed in one's official documents, as they are all interlinked and making a change in one means having to get it done on all documents across the board including the passport. When I asked her if many hijras and kotis feel similarly, and if there is any possibility she would change her mind later on, her response was as follows: the hijras and kotis most likely to change their gender on their documents are either the privileged ones who have contacts in the government and can get these changes done relatively easily, or the really poor ones who have the Aadhaar card as their only identity card and therefore find it easy to change their details on one document. Anybody with a network of interconnected identity cards and bank documents, including herself, would be unlikely to venture ahead and change their details – but of course, like everything else, such a decision is also dependent on one's personal choices and circumstances.

Hema's choice to retain her assigned gender in her official documents makes two powerful statements about subversion, agency and allyship. Her refusal to identify as 'female' in her official documents can be read as her recognition of the struggles of the ciswomen in the country for representation in government jobs, and her circumspection in taking a stand that avoids alienating potential allies from the transgender movement, which is also an ongoing struggle for visibility and representation in the government and in other domains of public life. However, Hema, who was born into a lower-caste family, has also refrained from drawing a caste certificate as a student and a professional. Her refusal to avail any kind of reservation (which she supports in principle) could be seen as her determination to proscribe any kind of discrimination or criticism regarding her merit or abilities (which she is used to fielding in the private and NGO sectors as a transfeminine person, where discrimination and monetary exploitation is rampant), and a desire to leave reserved seats open for those who need it more than she does.

Her weaponization of the gender identity saddled on her at birth to ensure that her social, professional and transnational mobility is not circumscribed in any way, on the other hand, is a powerful act of subversion and self-assertion – one that blurs any clearcut, dichotomous boundaries between (the gendered classification of) name, appearance and gender identity, and challenges the assumption that one's name or appearance must align with the gender one officially (or personally) identifies by.

Interestingly, Hema does not go by her natal surname in social circles any more, which is indicative of her lower-caste identity. Instead, she has adopted the surname of her *giriya* (husband), which happens to be a prestigious upper caste name, because she likes it and wants to be known by that name. For her, this is a means of exercising her agency to subvert the religious and legal structures that proscribe her right to marry a man by coopting a patriarchal convention prescribed by those very structures, which recommend that a married Hindu cisgender woman must change her surname to her husband's as a symbol of their marital bond.

This change also has the additional benefit of presenting her with some social capital and caste privilege that come with her new surname while subverting the traditional belief that someone born as a Hindu 'man' cannot change their caste identity, which a Hindu woman can through marriage.

## What's in a Name?

This impels us to consider the question: what does it mean for someone to have a name?

> To name a thing is to *acknowledge its existence* as separate from everything else that has a name; to confer upon it the *dignity of autonomy* while at the same time affirming its *belonging* with the rest of the namable world; to transform its strangeness into familiarity, which is the root of empathy. To name is *to pay attention*; to name is *to love*. Parents name their babies as a *first nonbiological marker of individuality* amid the human lot; lovers give each other private nicknames that sanctify their intimacy; it is only when we began naming domesticated animals that they stopped being animals and became pets. . . . And yet names are words, and words have a way of obscuring or warping the true meanings of their objects. (Popova 2015; emphasis added)

As Popova mentions, children are named at birth, which is one of the most fundamental ways of assigning gender to a child in most cultures. Their 'individuality', so to speak, is assigned to the child by external agents; whether they are comfortable with it or not determines a significant part of their life-journey. For young Arpit (alias Sheila), her given (masculine) name was a marker of her assigned gender – a gender she did not identify with. She did not feel that sense of 'belonging with the rest of the namable world' because her awareness of the gendered nature of her name (and the gender roles and expectations that come with it) kept her from relating to the world as herself – as an individual who was also a woman. Eventually, when she grew up, she chose a feminine name for herself, Sheila, to more closely reflect her sense of who she was and how she wanted to belong in the world. The act of (re) naming oneself is the ultimate assertion of one's individuality and agency, and for a trans person, it can mark a symbolic break from past lives, past names and past selves, and a rebirth into a new life, new body and new identity. In western queer discourse (that has gradually spread across the globe), the rejected birth name is called one's 'dead name', indicating a past self that is considered to be dead to the new, (often physically) transitioned self.

However, for Sheila, this act of naming herself did not entail the simultaneous rejection of her birth name for various practical reasons. Being a koti who studied in school and eventually college and who hoped to get a job in the mainstream world, instead of a hijra who intended to pursue traditional hijra occupations, the complete renunciation of everything that came with her previous name, including her family, her acquaintances, her degrees, her reputation and a certain symbolic association with her past life was neither a desirable nor a viable option for her. A koti's approach to their name, much like their bodies and lifestyles, is symptomatic of their role as people who embody multiple, fluid, sometimes conflicting identities within themselves, and exist in the liminal spaces between the mainstream and hijra worlds, traversing both with their own unique subjectivities.

Sheila's relationship with her name has since evolved, after she gained 'awareness' on issues of gender following various workshops and conversations she was privy to as a student and an activist – a change that is reflected in the attitudes of a few other kotis vis-à-vis their names. Instead of viewing a name as gendered, that consequently assigns the same gender to its referent, Sheila now considers a name to just be an identifying noun, to be stripped of its gendered connotations and considered an appropriate name for a person of any gender. She argues that it is the referent who attributes their gender feature to the name and not vice versa: thus, if Arpit identifies as a woman or a transgender, then the conventionally masculine name of Arpit – it logically follows – becomes a woman's or a transgender's name.

This reconceptualization of the relationship between name and gender is a radical intervention in the traditional discourse on gender and naming that has normalized the idea of names being gendered nouns, which are then used as tools to arbitrarily assign gender to newborns. Sheila's reconceptualization of her relationship with her name has the potential to revolutionize the trans discourse that aligns 'gendered' names with their corresponding 'gendered' bodies, suggesting instead that any process of physical transition into or embracing of one's gender identity need not necessarily entail a change in, or a rejection of, one's birth name on the grounds of its conventionalized gendered connotations. Within the community, this attitudinal and ideological shift from an understanding of gendered names as fixed, binary and immutable, to an understanding of names as changeable (in various ways) and of gender as a fluid spectrum that allows for shifting and plural expressions, has the potential to give many kotis the confidence to be comfortable with their birth names even as they publicly embrace their koti identities.

However, such ideological shifts are never neat and absolute (see Williams 1977). While Sheila insists on foregrounding the role of one's *karma* (actions) instead of one's name in shaping one's identity and reputation, she admits to pandering to conservative ideas of binary gender by using her feminine name when dealing with authority figures such as policemen, who would not take her seriously if she did not appear to be 'hijra-like enough'. Her manipulation of dominant ideological assumptions about hijras to make herself heard and acknowledged by those in power in order to fight for the needs and rights of the hijra-koti community is what ultimately gives her the power to earn the respect and goodwill of her community members, and to thus resignify the gendered connotations of her given name.

Sheila is one of very few kotis who is comfortable being addressed by either of her aliases. She feels that what she is called does not matter; what matters is whether or not she is respected. However, many hijras and kotis, especially those who are castrated, do not like to be addressed by their birth names, as those have long been used as a tool to insult and invalidate the feminine/femme identity of a hijra or koti by their gurus and peers (interview with Sheila; also see Hall and O'Donovan 1996). The connotations associated with a birth name are not just of gender, but also of deception and inauthenticity; convention dictates the need to publicly shed one's birth name and adopt a feminine name to finally be able to embrace one's 'true' and 'authentic' identity as a koti or a hijra. Yet, they do not object to being addressed by their nicknames like Tanu, Paku, Nani, irrespective of their gender connotations, because nicknames, especially in Bengal, signify a relationship of familiarity and intimacy that the referent shares with the interlocutor – a reflection of familial bonds that hijras and kotis perpetually seek to replicate, establish and nurture with each other.

In this context, Sheila and her peers' attempt to disrupt the expectation that a 'masculine' (formal) name must have a male referent is significant also because it disrupts the conventions and rhythms of the hijra-koti community as well as the mainstream community, in favour of a conceptualization of names as representational of the ambiguous and multiple gender identities of their referents.

One of the ways in which the ambiguity between one's gender identity, gender expression and gendered names finds expression in the larger hijra and koti community is in the way senior kotis are addressed by the younger ones. The convention where a masculine name combines with a masculine kinship term like *da* (elder brother) or *kaku* (uncle), as in Kishore *da* or Gopal *kaku*, and a feminine name combines with a feminine kinship term like *di* (elder sister) or *mashi* (aunt), as in Shobha *di* or Nupur *mashi*, is a predominant one in Bangla, and is duly followed in the hijra and koti communities too. If a koti is addressed by her masculine (given) name (irrespective of her gender presentation), the kinship term automatically attached with it is *da*, and when she is addressed by her feminine (or trans) name, the kinship term *di* is used with it. Very few people – whether within or outside the community – self-reflexively modify the conventions of the language to attach the term *di* with masculine or gender-neutral (nick)names, such as Argha and Banti, respectively, or the term *da* with feminine names such as Sheila. This practice is slowly gaining traction within the community as the idea of names being gender-agnostic gains more credence amongst its members. Yet, there remain loud and vehement voices that register their objection to the normalization of such a convention, arguing that if someone has chosen a feminine name for themselves in order to align with their identity as a transfeminine person, the respectful and validating thing to do would be to attach a feminine kinship term with that name, not a masculine one. The emergence of this linguistically and socially disruptive convention, while gradual, is exciting in its potential to lead to the interrogation and eventual reconceptualization of various ideas relating to gender and identity, including what it means to be a koti and what living one's life as a koti entails.

Meanwhile, the convention of addressing someone by their birth (male) name or a masculine kinship term is not approved of in hijra households, as induction into any hijra *gharana* is predicated on the symbolic renunciation of one's previous name, life, relationships and (masculine) identity, and the adoption of a new, feminine one. Notably, the only times a hijra is referred to or addressed by their birth name are if a past incident – when they still presented or identified as male – is recounted, or in order to humiliate and insult them for bad behaviour or for participating in some petty crime, like stealing. The rules are more flexible within the NGO sector, where kotis (and some hijras) feel comfortable to formally introduce themselves in meetings, etc., with both their birth and new names (as aliases), thereby highlighting the fluidity, ambiguity and multiplicity of their gender identities (field notes and interviews, 2017–20).

The effect of the binary framework by which natural gender is categorized in Bangla is so strong that despite real-life examples of people who consistently and variously challenge such neat categories of gender on a regular basis, speakers of Bangla (and Ulti) find it difficult to find terms of address that can appropriately give expression to the multiplicity of complex and fluid identities that the hijra-koti spectrum has to offer. Thereby, we see the limitations of a language like Ulti which came into being precisely to give expression to hijra-koti subjectivities that the dominant language and its speakers could not/would not accommodate, but fell short of being entirely representative of all of its speakers. Just as the gender system of any natural, organically growing language does not reflect the conceptual understanding of natural gender by its speakers, or the reality of gender plurality and representation in that society, so is it that a language like Ulti – albeit natural and growing itself – was developed consciously by a community of gender and sexual minorities to coin words to describe their specific subjectivities, inner worlds and experiences. Yet it is representative enough such that, merely through its existence, it challenges and subverts the hegemony of Bangla and the ideological imperatives that dominate and shape the culture of Bengal.

This convention of (mis)gendering people on the basis of their (gendered) names manifests itself even in multilingual contexts. In my early days of conducting this research, when I would talk about the community in English with fellow academics, I often found myself inadvertently referring to Hema, with a conventionally feminine name, with the feminine pronoun 'she', while Arpit, with a conventionally masculine name (which is used more commonly to refer to her than Sheila), would be referred to with the masculine pronoun 'he'. This, despite the fact that the gender expression and presentation of both these persons, including their hair and clothes, were almost identical in their androgyny tending towards femininity (except on occasions when they would dress up in beautiful sarees, with full make-up and jewellery). This problem would not arise when I would speak of them in Bangla because it contains no gendered pronouns, thereby liberating the speakers from the responsibility of assigning a gender to anybody – whether in the first or the third person – while referring to them(selves). However, in my native language Sylheti, which like English contains gendered third person pronouns, this problem would resurface.

Upon introspection, it was clear that the only reason my brain would make these pronoun choices while speaking unchecked was because it associated certain traditional genders with certain names, and despite knowing that these particular names referred to transfeminine people who did not fit into traditional categories of gender, the linguistic constraints presented by languages like English and Sylheti necessitated that speakers make a gendered choice of pronoun if they want to refer to a person in an informal manner. Selecting the gender most conventionally associated with the name as default is almost instinctive for any native or near-native speaker of these languages, thus running the curious risk of misgendering a person in a language they probably do not speak or understand.

However, instincts can be changed; after innumerable slip-ups and constant self-correction, my brain – and consequently my tongue – has now reached a stage where it can refer to an Arpit as a 'she' in both English and Sylheti without conscious self-intervention. Speakers of Ulti, being mostly native Bangla speakers, typically do not worry about what their pronouns are or have rigid stances about them the way non-binary people in the west or English-speaking persons in India do, because for them, pronouns are not relevant or culturally significant linguistic devices to refer to their gender(s). However, how such different experiences and expressions of gender can be translated into other languages – some with very different grammatical parameters, including a lack of a gender-neutral animate pronoun – in culturally diverse, multilingual environments, is a metalinguistic question that needs to be examined in greater detail.

## Language, Discrimination and Intersectional Identities

The hijra-koti community has a very layered, multifaceted and unique relationship with language, aspects of which have been discussed in the previous chapter as well as this one. The community thrives in a rich multilingual ecology that includes Ulti and other languages spoken in the region, such as Bangla, (some of) its regional varieties, and some degree of Hindi and English. The community members – the speech community of Ulti – hail from various linguistic and socioeconomic backgrounds which determine, to a large extent, the languages they have access to and the levels of proficiency they might typically achieve in each language.

It is important to note here that this community is different from other speech communities in that Ulti does not function as anybody's first language or home language. Ulti is a sociolect that is spoken exclusively by the community members, and since they each have different first languages and are introduced to the community at various stages much later in their lives, Ulti is never acquired as a first language by anybody. Even if a child is adopted by a hijra, they would grow up speaking the first language of their adoptive mother, because the domains in which Ulti is used do not include every domain of the hijra's life. Just as hijras and kotis frequently speak in Bangla even within the community to talk about the wide range of topics that Ulti has no lexical items for, so too, for similar reasons, they would speak to their children in their first language or home language.

Therefore, the language that a hijra or a koti speaks has a strong influence on how they speak Ulti. As has been mentioned in the previous chapter, the matrix language of Ulti is standard Bangla, but many varieties of Ulti occur where the matrix language is any other variety of Bangla, making the linguistic behaviour of the community very heterogenous due to the varied linguistic influences that characterize them. For the purposes of this research, I have limited my study to the variety most widely spoken in the region which has standard Bangla as its matrix language.

The linguistic profile of the Ulti speech community is a product of their intersectional identities, which determine their position in society and their ability to access various kinds of linguistic, ideological, cultural, political and financial resources to move up in society and secure better lives for themselves and the community. The community is composed of a diverse set of people, most of whom occupy a cumulatively lower status in society owing to being systematically marginalized along multiple axes of identity – class, caste, geography (rural or suburban), gender and sexual identity. The class, caste and geographical location of a koti determines the quality and level of education, as well as the medium of instruction they have access to, while their gender identity and sexual preferences often become the reason they are bullied and harassed into dropping out of school in their teenage years (discussed later in this chapter).

The norm in the districts of Nadia and North 24 Parganas, where this particular speech community resides, is to send children from lower-income families to Bangla-medium schools, as they are more affordable and accessible than the English-medium ones. Most of the community come from ethnically Bengali native or immigrant families who either speak standard Bangla or one of its regional varieties as their first language or home language. The dominant variety of Bangla, which is taught in schools and spoken across the region, has emerged as the contact language for these immigrants, who aspire to have their children assimilate into this language and culture. The ethnically non-Bengali immigrants in the region, like the Nepalis, Biharis, Punjabis and Marwaris, likewise speak their native languages at home but prefer to send their children to Hindi- or English-medium schools, because those are the languages of trade, of intra-national and international contact, and of upward professional and social mobility.

Significantly, the hijra-koti community has very few Nepali and Bihari members, who invariably hail from lower-class families, and no Punjabi and Marwari members, which could be attributed to their economic class, which plays a key role in separating them from the hijra-koti community by giving them access to more upper-class, urbane, English-speaking queer spaces in Kolkata and on social media. It is the same with upper-class and upper-caste queer Bengali people who define their gender and sexual identities based on a western framework of queer identities, have access to queer spaces where they can express themselves freely, have access to professions and locations where they can live their lives in relative comfort and safety, have access to literature and audio-visual content in English (and other languages, subtitled in or translated to English) – that help them validate and come to terms with their identities and experiences, and thereby create elite, urbane queer communities that symbolically and materially distance themselves from the hijra and koti communities at various levels. Just as gaining access to a global language like English as a child significantly defines the life-experiences of the urban queer community, the overwhelming lack of it defines the life-experiences of the hijra and koti community in equally significant ways.

An interesting insight into the community's relationship with the written word can be gained from a look at their social media behaviour. A hijra-koti WhatsApp group with nearly 130 members reveals that most of their interactions happen via three forms of media: visual (pictures), audio-visual (videos) and audio (self-recorded voice messages and songs, mostly in Bangla and Ulti). Text messages are negligible, and most of those that do appear are in Bangla, written mostly in the Bangla and occasionally the Roman script. Given that a large number of community members are unlettered or school dropouts, these modes of communication act as levelling grounds where everyone can participate in the conversations as equals, irrespective of their educational or linguistic backgrounds. The language of choice in these interactions is mostly Bangla, with Ulti being spoken whenever the context calls for it. On dating apps, the language of choice is purely functional: it consists of a set of abbreviated codes in English common to the domain and oriented towards meeting a short-term sexual partner, like 'top', 'bottom', 'ASL' (age, sex, location) and so on. On more social sites like Facebook, the language of choice is typically Bangla, written in either the Bangla or the Roman script.

Most speakers of Ulti, therefore, are fluent in standard Bangla and conversant in Hindi with varying degrees of fluency. Bangla, after Ulti, is the language of interpersonal communication within the community, as well as the language (not so closely followed by Hindi) in which much of the professional and personal communication between hijras/kotis and the mainstream community takes place, from negotiations during *badhai* to flirting with a lover to conversations with one's biological family. Many hijras and kotis also choose to express their deepest emotions and subjectivities through older Bangla and Hindi songs about love, yearning, heartbreak and devotion, which they share with their peers on WhatsApp groups as well as perform on formal occasions. Their exposure to English is mostly restricted to preliminary English lessons in school and content on social media and popular culture, which gives them a very limited degree of competence in the language. This reality is reflected by the Ulti words that refer to Bangla and English, which are *amago khutni* ('our words/language') and *ariyal khutni* ('big words/language'), respectively. They reveal a perceptual distance the community experiences with each of these languages corresponding to how accessible they each are for a large section of the community, and how they emotionally respond to each language as either intimate or intimidating.

English is the lingua franca of the urban, metropolitan queer community, and it has been used by them as a means of othering the non-English-speaking, economically, socially and regionally disadvantaged hijra-koti community, and limit their access to power, resources and representation within the larger queer community. Thus, the English-speaking queer circles have distanced themselves from the community and are consequently regarded with scorn by many, though some others do aspire to emulate them. The English language, therefore, is now selectively and strategically utilized by the community in order to spread awareness amongst community members about issues related to their sexual health, human rights, sexuality and gender, to share news about and generate funds for community-based welfare activism with people in the mainstream, and to engage in sociopolitical discourse surrounding the community.

The above-mentioned process of othering the community based on their class, caste and geographical location in the non-profit sector was discussed in detail on a panel entitled 'Discrimination and Nepotism in the LGBTQIA Movement' on 2 August 2020,[1] where North Bengal-based trans activist Sumi Das called out the rhetoric of the trans community not being fragmented along caste lines as 'fake'. She points out the casteism and exclusion inherent in the composition of the Transgender Development Board, and highlights the 'us vs. them' sentiment that characterizes much of the treatment meted out by the elite, urban non-profit sector to the disadvantaged, rural hijra-koti communities. They are discriminated against based on their 'hijra-like' appearance, style, choice of outfits (saree), etc., which are markers of their class and regional location, and thus excluded from decision-making processes and representation at various levels.

Sumi and Sheila also reveal the entrenched corruption in the former, whose project leaders would pay members of the latter a fraction of their salary in some HIV projects while having them sign documents that claimed they had received the full amount, thus making it impossible for them to justifiably claim that they had been wronged. Sumi further shares that '*jara nichu jat-er chilo sei office e tader cha-er cup, bhat-er thala obdi alada thakto onek somoy . . . tara bosbe hoyto onno jaygate*' ('the lower-caste staff in that office had separate cups and plates . . . they were made to sit separately from everyone else'). This reveals that the Brahminical concepts of purity and contamination that the caste system is built upon is perpetuated even in such 'woke', educated circles that claim to be 'progressive'. As a result, many kotis permanently left the non-profit sector and began to earn their living by going for *lagans*[2] in Uttar Pradesh (U.P.) and Bihar with fellow hijras and kotis.

Similar forms of caste-based discrimination also take place within the hijra-koti community itself, despite the efforts of community members to eradicate such forms of discriminatory thought and practice within the community. One such instance occurred when the community members were invited to a funeral ceremony in a hijra household, where the hosts refused to serve food to a couple of lower-caste hijras citing reasons of impurity, which was then met with loud objections by the other guests. While the community constantly strives to be a place of true equality and unconditional acceptance for everyone, the ideological framework with which members of the community grew up (before entering the community and engaging in discourses that challenged their set beliefs on many issues) are often hard to come to terms with and eventually break away from, resulting in the replication of dominant patterns of discriminatory thought and behaviour within the community. As the Dalit trans activist Grace Banu G (2020) put it in quite a different context, 'Casteism, Brahminism, permeates the trans community and infects it with its transphobia.'[3]

One such form of discrimination emerges from entrenched ideas about what constitutes femininity, and the censure directed at those who do not comply with those standards. Whether it is a koti who wears a saree and make-up while sporting a beard, or a koti who is in a relationship with another koti instead of the expected male *panthi* or *parik* (lover), many members of the community find it difficult to accept them as 'true' hijras or kotis who are expected to aspire to the 'sacred' ideal of feminine *shringaar* ('aesthetics and adornment') and experiencing only heterosexual attraction ('we are women, we must love men, it is only "natural"'). The predominant ideal of femininity within the community is borrowed from mainstream constructs of binary gender and heterosexual desire, even though the language of Ulti as well as their lived realities indicate a much wider spectrum of (feminine) experiences and subjectivities.

The hegemony of dominant discourses permeates the community at every level, as can be expected given the immersion of the community members in their natal cultures and ideologies. This discourse is countered by emerging voices committed to the ideals of equality and acceptance and exposed to the concept of gender and sexual fluidity, who point out the hypocrisy inherent in the act of perpetuating dominant forms of discrimination within the community by those who have been targets of such behaviour themselves. The language of these alternative discourses that emerge from within the community varies: while they may be expressed in Bangla on occasion, they are most potent when expressed in Ulti.

Ulti is one of the primary markers of membership in the hijra-koti community. It is the language through which the community and concepts of gender and sexuality are first introduced to young kotis, and the language through which they undertake a journey of self-discovery, forge bonds of companionship and solidarity with fellow hijras and kotis, and consolidate their position within the community with growing fluency in the language. It is a prestige language and carries a lot of linguistic capital; fluency in Ulti indexes one's seniority, power and authority, and commands great respect within the community.

It is a marker of hijra and koti identity – the language that gives voice to their subjectivities, desires, experiences and lived reality. It defines the structures, relationships and occupations that shape the hijra social system, thus giving them the legitimacy and 'dignity of autonomy' (Popova 2015) that the process of naming imparts on its referents. Hence, it is the language that made it possible for hijras to organize themselves into a distinct social group which then became a haven for generations of kotis – abandoned by their families and shunned by society – where they found refuge, an alternative family, and a social system which would enable them to earn their living and thrive amongst people like themselves while being free to present and express themselves as the gender they identify with.

The status of Ulti as a marker of hijra-koti identity is the reason many hijras and koti object to the idea of a *parik* – a cisgender man – speaking the language (which they might have learnt from their long-term, live-in koti partners), as they consider it a violation of their privacy, an intrusion into their inner discursive world. Interestingly, it is not considered equally objectionable when ciswomen (like me) speak Ulti, because women are seen as their natural allies by hijras and kotis, who have traditionally aspired to align their femme/feminine identity with an ideal of binary, cisgender femininity, which is reflected in their gender behaviour. Thus, Ulti is symbolically considered to be a feminine language, meant to be spoken exclusively by feminine/femme persons and kept away from their cisgender heterosexual lovers. However, community members are not opposed to gay and bisexual men – who are part of the larger queer community and spend some time with hijras and kotis – acquiring some level of proficiency in Ulti, as they are also seen as allies due to their shared interest in and attraction to cisgender men.

The following excerpt from a conversation with a senior koti, Bijoli (B), illustrates some of the points discussed above. 'E' refers to this author.

Excerpt 2

B: *Kotider bhasha kotira . . . tonnara bolle kemon lage, tahole to tonnara koti-i hoye gelo na?*
E: *To amra bolle?*
B: *Tomra thik acho, tomra to meye, amader bandhobir moto, tomader kono problem nei. Chhelera bolle ektu bicchiri lage dekhte, tahole to tomar – chhupiye rekhe chheleder saamne kono kichu kotha bola jabena, na? Ulti bhashata keno boli . . . jate tonnara kichu na bojhe, oder saamne oder bodnam kora jabe . . . er jonnei to Ulti bhashatar proyog hoy.*

Translation

B: Kotis should speak their [language] . . . it's weird when men speak it, then the man just becomes a koti, isn't it?
E: And if we speak it?
B: You all are fine, you are women, you're like our friends, you are not a problem. But it looks bad when men speak it, because then you'll not be able to say anything secret in front of them, right? Why do we speak Ulti . . . so that men don't understand anything, and we can insult them to their faces . . . that is why we use Ulti. (Interview with Bijoli)

While Ulti has always been closely guarded by the community as an exclusive, secret language, divulging information about it to very few outsiders to ensure their safety and privacy, it does not function as the lingua franca of the community. Its use is limited by the domains (to be elaborated upon in the next chapter) it is used in, i.e. Ulti cannot be used to talk about topics for which there are no Ulti lexical items. This necessitates that Bangla, the dominant language of the region and the first language of many in the community, also be commonly used in hijra-koti circles. While the domains of use of Ulti and Bangla are fairly distinct, there exist many domains which contain both Ulti and Bangla lexical items (such as food, clothes, make-up, money, etc.). The choice of language in these conversational contexts is determined by a number of factors. In a conversation taking place in safe intra-community spaces such as someone's house, NGO quarters or private social media groups, Ulti is used often and with flourish alongside Bangla. Conversations with community outsiders are mostly held in Bangla or other contact languages; it is only a few trusted friends and allies of community members who are privy to the existence of Ulti and have been taught a small set of words in the language.

However, contrary to expectation, one of the most important spaces in which Ulti is used is the liminal spaces that constitute the interfaces between the community and the mainstream. All traditional hijra occupations involve verbal interaction between the hijras and their clients. While direct conversations in such contexts take place in Bangla, any conversation involving the specifics of the job amongst the hijras takes place in Ulti, often in front of the clients themselves. It is important to note that the names of the hijra occupations like *badhai*,[4] *cholla*[5] and *khajra*,[6] as well as other words related to them including denominations of money, are coined in Ulti, which makes the use of the language imperative apart from lending the speakers with a convenient device to camouflage the contents of their conversation in plain sight. Ulti is also used by hijras and kotis to scrutinize and discuss the appearance of potential love interests in their vicinity, as well as to warn each other of danger when they spy policemen approaching while they are cruising the streets for clients. The community does not seem much concerned about protecting Ulti from discovery by the mainstream; rather, they enjoy using Ulti to tease and defy the mainstream without them realizing it, and wielding it as a linguistic shield to protect themselves from the harassment and exploitation they have come to anticipate in many situations. Thus we see how the existence of Ulti does not automatically entail the rejection of Bangla by the speech community; they coexist in linguistic collusion with each other and the other languages spoken by the community.

There has been substantial debate in the literature about code-switching or language-switching between two varieties, and the reasons why a speaker might switch languages during a conversation. 'Conversational code switching can be defined as the juxtaposition within the same speech exchange of passages of speech belonging to two different grammatical systems or subsystems' (Gumperz 1982: 59). It must be noted that the switch between Ulti and Bangla does not qualify as code-switching as defined by Gumperz, who argued that 'codeswitching takes place when the grammatical systems of both languages (as well as the words) are used in the same exchange' (Paolillo 2011: 2, paraphrasing Gumperz 1982). He distinguishes it from borrowing, which 'occurs when a language adopts words or other elements from another language and incorporates them into its existing grammar' (ibid.). Neither of these structural distinctions take into account a language like Ulti which is neither just a case of Ulti words being borrowed by Bangla, nor a case of code-switching between two languages which possess original and separate grammars of their own. Ulti is a sociolect that has Bangla as its matrix language and functions as a separate language variety. Keeping this in mind, the term 'language-switching' is most appropriate when discussing switches in conversation between Ulti and Bangla.

Blom and Gumperz (1972) distinguish between two forms of language-switching: situational and metaphorical. They posit that the idea of situational switching presumes that there is a direct relationship between language and the social situation with a shift in social situation entailing a switch in the language or variety used, while metaphorical switching is characterized by a shift in the language used for no perceptible reason other than the will of the speaker. This shift, argue Blom and Gumperz, has a 'semantic effect' on the conversation because every language has a value attached to it, and a shift from one to the other indexes subtle shifts in speaker attitude and interactional meaning in the conversation, such as inviting confidences, exercising authority, etc.

In the case of Ulti and Bangla, shifts between the two languages can be characterized as either situational or metaphorical depending on the context in which they occur. In mainstream spaces, the shift is often situational, motivated by the people present around the interlocutors, the topic, as well as the location itself. Amongst community insiders, however, Ulti and Bangla are often used freely and interchangeably, such that any shift (that is not dependent on a shift to a domain-specific topic exclusive to one of the languages) can be read as metaphorical in nature, meant to index the familiarity, solidarity and companionship shared by community insiders with each other. However, as Auer warns us:

> There is a certain danger . . . to treat each and every instance of language alternation as meaningful in the same 'semantic' way. Such a view does not take

> into account that it is not the mere fact of the juxtaposition of two languages that makes relevant something like 'meanings' attached to these languages in the semantic sense. Code-switching may be functional without having a semantic meaning of this type. (Auer 1984b: 105)

Issues related to code-switching and bilingualism in Ulti and Bangla will be further discussed in chapter 4.

## Community Membership

The hijra-koti community is open, fluid and very accepting of anyone who identifies as or seems to be a koti. Being intimately acquainted with the pressures of growing up as an effeminate or trans child in conservative households, senior kotis who have assimilated into the community often identify them in public places or are introduced to them by common friends, and, upon getting to know them better, introduce them to the community and suggest that they might be kotis as well. The community thus spans a wide variety of gender/sexual identities, from gay and effeminate men to trans women, closeted to openly feminine hijras and kotis, and a broad spectrum of subjectivities in between. Many community members may be questioning, uncomfortable or coming to terms with their identities, while others are figures of authority and trust who are actively involved in community-related activities and endeavour to support and take care of each community member, however integrated they might (or might not) be into the community. The fulcrum of these activities is the Nadia Ranaghat Sampriti Society, a non-profit organization run by community insiders to work for the welfare of the hijra-koti community of Nadia and its neighbouring districts.

The community, thus, poses no restrictions upon its membership beyond one's (possible) identity as a gender-queer, non-heterosexual individual. One's choice to identify as a community member is not something that is taken into account, as 'community' in this context is a very abstract concept of a social group, not an organization of any kind; a community member, hence, is one who is or seems to be a koti, whether or not they want to be part of the community themselves. However, given its status as a cumulatively marginalized group, this community is frequently discriminated against and shunned by queer personalities and groups who occupy more privileged positions in society. These lines are most often drawn along the axes of caste, class and location.

One of the most famous personalities to have emerged out of the Nadia-based community has been hailed as the first transgender college principal in India. She identified as koti and dhurani in the past, but now identifies as transgender. She used to be immersed in Ulti and hijra-koti culture, and continues to stay in touch with her *gotiya* ('sister/co-*caela* under the same guru'), a prominent community senior, but upon gaining privilege, national renown and class mobility, she has consciously distanced herself from the community and never speaks about them in public. Many members of the community resent the fact that having risen to prominence by virtue of her transgender identity, she has not used her platform to generate the much-needed attention, funds and resources to uplift and support her fellow hijras and kotis.

Such resentment is also directed toward a prominent (now deceased) filmmaker based in Kolkata, though to a much lesser degree. This filmmaker presented as effeminate and gender-queer without explicitly coming out and identifying as transgender or koti or anything else, but the embodied shifts in their gender presentation became an inalienable part of their public persona and narrative, finding expression in their only films as an actor which were made in the last years of their life. The presence of such a prominent, respected, well-loved, gender-queer, transfemme celebrity persona played a huge role in imbuing the figure of the hijra and the koti with the humanity and relatability that the mainstream society had failed to see in them for generations. The community members also saw in this person a reflection of themselves, which shored up their sense of self-worth, confidence, validation and comfort in one's body and gender identity to no mean degree. However, there is also a sense of having been let down by them because they, too, have never spoken for or worked to ensure the well-being of the hijra-koti community in particular. Their gender politics and representation of queerness in their cinema was also mediated through lenses determined by their (upper) class, caste and metropolitan position.

However, upward social mobility or a privileged class and caste position does not always entail rejection and othering of the community by fellow kotis or transpersons. There are US-based academics, activists, advocates, judges and a few other figures, who have earned fame and success in the larger queer community and in their respective fields, who have dedicated their lives to working and advocating for the rights and representation of the hijra-koti community, and who are thereby held in very high esteem by the community members.

## The Life of a Koti

Young, pre-pubescent kotis (who do not identify as kotis yet) grow up in families, neighbourhoods and schools surrounded by people – young and old – who are steeped in the hegemonic ideals of the dominant community that they hail from or aspire to, which makes them intolerant of any deviation from the norm in anyone's gender expression and sexual preferences. This predisposition, exacerbated by the complete lack of awareness on the issue of sexual and gender diversity, gives rise to a school system where teachers are not equipped to be sensitive to the needs of gender-diverse children. This makes young effeminate boys the target of verbal, mental and sexual harassment and abuse from their peers as well as seniors and authority figures, which they find themselves unable to report to anyone for fear that nobody would believe them if they did, which leaves them open to further bullying and abuse, leading to depression, isolation, helplessness and inability to focus their energies on their education or form deep, trusting, meaningful bonds with most cisgender and heterosexual people around them. Sheila, now an influential koti in the region, regretfully recounts how her grades plummeted when she moved from primary to middle school, in class 5, when she first began to suffer sexual abuse at the hands of her peers.

Born into a lower middle-class Brahmin family, Sheila remembers herself as a child who loved to fashion herself after her mother instead of her father, as most young boys are wont to do. Playing with dolls and kitchen sets, draping herself in her mother's sarees, wearing nail polish – essentially replicating the gender expression and roles her mother would perform – would give her the most joy as a child. But what was indulged in a child was not tolerated in an adult. Her father would frequently tell her that it was not acceptable for her to be a koti because they were Brahmins; '"they" [referring to her koti companions] can be like "that" [indicating her long hair and feminine clothes]', he would say, 'but this can never happen in my house'. She was discouraged from attending a cousin's wedding unless she cut her hair short – the family's prestige was at stake – but when she started gifting them gold rings on their weddings, nobody openly criticized the hair any more. She recounts her childhood thus:

Excerpt 3

*Jokhon boro hocchi tokhon aste-aste dekhchi je amar bhalo laga ta hocche putul khela, luko-churi khela, saat-chara khela. Amar bhalo laga hocche mohila der sathe khela . . . ei niye thaktam. Hoyto seikhane amar bhai ba amar dadara dekha jacche just cricket khelche, jeta 'tonna-pon' er khela. To ami sekhane laharan-pon er khela gulo khelchilam, se gulo suddha-suddhi-der prothome opochondo hote shuru holo.*

*Tokhoni erokomo hoyeche je school er teacher ba tuition er teacher bolche je 'o jodi cricket khelto or mostishko ta clear hoto. Oke cricket khelay bhorti korun'. Se khetre ami erokomo dekhechi je bari theke amake gymnastics e bhorti korechilo. To gymnastic e korte giye ghare baetha lege gelo hothat kore. To sei khetre ami bhablam je 'hai re, ami je ki korte ki korlam re!' Choto bela theke tokhon nijer bhul ta proman hoye jete thake je aajke . . . amra je choto bela thekei nijeke je alada kore rakha, ba amra je bhul, amra je ei somaje ektu-ektu alada – seta nijer baba ma kintu phutiye tulto. Jodi amader baba ma jodi bolto je 'tui eta khelchish etai khel . . . etai tor bhalo laga', tahole hoyto amar moddhe . . . aro egiye jete partam onno kichu niye.*

*Jokhon ami jei khela ta khelchi setai jokhon bhul tokhon mone hocche 'tale ami ki khelbo, konta sothik?' Amra sekhanei confusion hoye pori; je amader confusion ta thake, 'tale amader sothik ta konta?' Cricket khela, kintu cricket khela ta to dekhlam tonnara khelche, baetha lagche, douracche . . . aar ami to putul khelte bhalo bashtam, ami naach korte bhalo bashtam. Amar bhalo laga thakto naach. Tai boddhota hoye baba ekbar naache o bhorti koralo. Kintu ki bolbo, mane bhaggo krome, naacher oikhane jawa holo na kenona attiyo-sojonra bollo je naache gele beshi 'ladies' ba beshi mouga type er hoye jabe. To naach bondho hoye gelo.*

Translation

When I was growing up, I began to realize that the things I liked to do were to play with dolls, play hide-and-seek, seven stones. I liked to play with girls. I was immersed in all this. Meanwhile, my brothers were seen to be playing just cricket, which is a 'masculine' sport. Since I was playing 'feminine' games, my parents began to dislike my pursuits for the first time.

Around the same time, my school and tuition teachers suggested that 'if he played cricket his mind would be clear. Make him join cricket'. Subsequently, I was made to join gymnastics, but soon I suffered a neck injury. I thought to myself, 'Oh god, what did I do!' Thus, from my childhood, it would seem like everything was a proof of my mistakes . . . from a young age, the fact that we would isolate ourselves from everyone, that we were always wrong, that we were slightly different from this society – these things would be highlighted and held up before us by our own parents. Had our parents told us instead, 'play what you are playing, if that's what you like', then perhaps we would have been able to move ahead in life with something else.

> When the game I'm playing itself is wrong, then one feels, 'then what should I play, what is right?' That's where we get confused: 'what is right for us?' Cricket, yes, but I would see boys playing cricket, getting hurt, running . . . and I liked to play with dolls. I liked to dance. Hence, defeated, my father even enrolled me into dance classes. But what do I say, as luck would have it, I could not attend the dance classes because our relatives said that if I dance I'll become even more girlish or effeminate. Thus, the dance classes had to stop. (Interview with Sheila)

In this excerpt, Sheila relays in detail the psychological and emotional confusion and pain experienced by a young child caught between gender roles. These gender roles are exclusive, drawn along binary frames of gender, and play a major role in socializing children into the gender roles they are expected to grow into. In the event where a child's likes, wants and desires are seen to be at odds with societal expectations, they are pressured by various 'benevolent' elements, beginning with the parents, to conform to the expected ideals. The child's body, psyche and actions are all labelled 'wrong' by authority figures surrounding them, which the child perceives as a character judgement and internalizes it, leading to long-term psychological effects as well as body and gender dysmorphia in many cases.

Sheila notes that many kotis would have not wasted valuable time questioning and worrying about what they must do to 'fit in' if only they had been accepted and supported by their parents for being themselves; they would instead have invested that time in the pursuit of their hobbies and goals, and would probably have achieved a great deal more than they have managed to at present. She goes on to talk about the kotis who have succumbed to suicide or run away from home as a result of growing up in such repressed environments, and points out that if any koti or hijra has managed to achieve something after coming from such backgrounds, they have done so after overcoming a lot of practical, social and psychological obstacles, which is a feat of strength and courage not everyone is capable of, which is why they are limited to occupations and lifestyles limited to the hijra-koti circle of trade.

As a student Sheila (then known only as Arpit) says she liked to study, would score well in school and rank amongst the top five in her class. But her effeminate tendencies attracted the attention of the boys in school, who would harass her, follow her to the toilets and ask if she had gotten rid of her penis. One day, when she was in class 5, a bunch of them accosted her and wrote the word 'homo' on her penis. This incident left a lasting scar on her psyche;

she felt like she had been branded with the slur. Terms like 'homo', 'item song', 'boudi' (brother's wife; used as a misogynistic and homophobic slur in the region) and 'hijra', which would often be directed at her, intensified this sensation of being branded. She says that the motivation behind the abuse was the attempt of her abusers to prove their masculinity before the girls and boys in their class; this same politics of masculinity was probably also responsible for keeping the more masculine senior trans children from paying any attention to her or supporting her in her struggles, thus aggravating her depression and loneliness. Her only companions in school as well as college were cisgender girls, who would find her company safe and reassuring for a 'boy'.

Her romantic relationships have also been similarly doomed. Most men, in her experience, prefer to get involved with kotis in clandestine affairs, and end up using them emotionally and sexually. They are not considered viable options for long-term love, relationships and marriage; their lovers do not even like to be seen associating with them in public spaces and social events. Sheila describes herself as a 'use and throw' item in her relationships, despite how much love and devotion she may have showered on her *parik*. Today, Sheila feels like she is a failure just because of her experiences as a transgender, despite the considerable success, respect and power she has attained within and outside the community for her work as a student leader and social activist. In her words, that respect follows the political power she has attained, the contacts she has made and the work she has put in as a leader. Yet, she was not considered eligible to be nominated as a candidate for her college elections by her party because: 'Do we now have to put up with the likes of you as our leader? What next?'

Another common source of abuse in schools and colleges is the absence of transgender toilets. If an effeminate boy or a transfeminine or femme person goes to the boys' toilet, they are harassed and ridiculed to such an extent that many prefer not to visit the toilet for the entire duration they are in school, which could span eight to nine hours, while if they visit the girls' toilet, they are viewed as perverts, voyeurs and a threat to the girls. The health hazards due to not being willing or able to access the toilet for such long spans of time on a daily basis also plays a huge role in causing these children to drop out from school in such large numbers, especially in their teenage years when the attention and the abuse intensify. Significantly, in 2017, Sheila was instrumental in getting a transgender toilet – the second of its kind to be installed in a government educational institution in India – installed at the local college she graduated from, so as to prevent current and future koti students from dropping out for similar reasons.

Besides the absence of safe or transgender toilets, the abuse and psychological trauma that many hijras and kotis suffer growing up in such conservative and repressed environments also contribute to the high rate of school drop-outs in the community. Many of these children meet senior, *bhelki* ('out') hijras and kotis on the streets, in parks and at festivals like the Neel Naach,[7] where they first begin to discover and understand not only their own gender identity and sexual orientation, but also that there are other such people in the world and that it is 'normal' to be this way. These senior community members first introduce them to Ulti and the ways of the community; over time, they stay in touch, support each other, advise each other on the ways in which they can safely undergo a bodily transformation (via counselling, hormone treatment, laser surgery and sex reassignment surgery) if they so wish, and thereby build a network of relationships within the community that gives them the space and the voice to express themselves in a way that has not been available to them outside of this community.

## The Hijra Lifestyle

The guru–*caela* ('master–disciple') system lies at the heart of the hijra *gharana*[8] and forms the spine of the hijra social system. There are more than seven major hijra *gharana*s in the subcontinent which act as the power centres of the hijra ecosystem; every hijra household or *daiyar* in the subcontinent is a part of one of these *gharana*s. A hijra household usually houses a guru and a few of her *caela*s, who are meant to serve her, take care of the household and accompany her on *toli-badhai*s, where they earn their living by going to houses who have recently welcomed newborns or newly-weds, and singing, dancing and blessing them to celebrate the auspicious occasion, receiving a lot of *joubon* ('gifts and money') in return.

There are many ways in which a guru selects a *caela*. In certain cases, a koti can express their wish to join a hijra house – as a means to enable them to escape their abusive and repressive household, or simply because they want to integrate further into the community. In other cases, the presence of a koti in the neighbourhood who has begun to keep her hair long and wear feminine clothing and accessories might engender fears of 'fake' hijras (boys being converted by the 'real' hijras) among the locals, which might then have an adverse effect on the income and the trust and respect the hijras of the area can continue to earn. To pre-empt such an eventuality, a guru might urge a koti to join her household and present herself in more traditionally feminine ways so that they can share the earnings from the area and ensure the safety and well-being of everyone involved. While the decision to join a hijra *gharana* is, at its core, a voluntary one taken by a koti, the koti herself does not get to select her guru; it is always the other way around.

The process of initiation into a hijra household involves two major steps: *ancla deoa* and *reet dhala.* The first involves a ceremony where the guru drapes her *ancal* (end of a saree or a dupatta) over the new *caela*'s head and feeds them *laddoo*s (a type of sweet) served on a *pan* (betel leaf). The second involves the payment of a nominal amount as security money by the *caela* to the guru (*reet*) who wants to take a *caela*, called *reet dhala* ('giving *reet*'), and the utterance, 'From today, [they] become a *caela* in my name' before an audience. This ceremony, performed by a guru, signifies the moment from when a *caela* becomes a part of the guru's household. This is also the moment a koti formally becomes a hijra, though which term a *caela* chooses to identify themselves by depends on many contingent factors, not least of which is whether they choose to live with the guru or continue to live with their natal families.

While the traditional custom of acquiring a *caela* involved the *caela* moving into the guru's house and staying there until they became a guru themselves and acquired *caela*s of their own years later, recent changes in the socioeconomic conditions of the country – which will be elaborated upon later – have precipitated sudden and frequent shifts in the hijra landscape, as an indirect result of which many *caela*s now live at different locations from their gurus. For similar reasons of strategic expediency, the customs of *ancla deoa* and *reet dhala* which are meant to happen in conjunction with each other, can sometimes take place on different occasions, years apart from each other. However, such occurrences are the exception rather than the norm.

The hijra gharana acts as an alternative family unit characterized by very rigid hierarchies. The *caela* addresses their hijra guru as *ma* ('mother'), while the guru recognizes their *caela* as their daughter. The guru of the guru is known as the *nanguru*; the *caela* addresses her as *nani* ('mother's mother'). The guru of the *nanguru* is known as the *dadguru*, whom the *caela* calls *dadi* ('father's mother'). The *caela* of one's *caela* becomes one's *nati caela* ('grand-*caela* [M]'), while the other *caela*s of one's guru becomes their *gotiya* ('sister'). The *gotiya* of one's guru is referred to as one's *khaliya* guru (mother's sister). Interestingly, the short forms of the kinship terms used to address various members of the hijra family unit (such as *ma*, *nani*, *dadi*) come from biological kinship terms in many Indo-Aryan languages, while the full terms themselves seem to have been coined by the hijra community. Further, barring *nati caela*, most of the other terms of address refer to close female relationships within the biological family, indicating that the hijra family structure – while being modelled on the traditional family structure – emphatically intends to subvert the gendered power dynamics of the patriarchal family. The hijra family structure also subverts the foundational concept of the patriarchal family that families can be made only through blood and marriage, by creating a diverse, plural, chosen family that is bound by neither blood nor marriage.

Besides these kinship terms, the other terms that are important in the hijra hierarchy have to do with profession, position and power. Most hijra gurus are *badhai-ali* hijras, who would only do *badhai* in designated areas with their *caela*s. Those areas are called *dera*s (a collection of *para birid*s or neighbourhood localities) whose heads are *daradin*s – often the guru themselves. A large area with a bunch of *dera*s is headed by a *naek*, while a larger area that has a bunch of areas under *naek*s is called a *birid*, which usually comprises a large town or a group of two to three smaller towns. A senior *naek*, who heads the *birid* and has the power to supervise and judge disputes between a set of younger *naek*s, is known as the *kundi*. At the top of the hierarchy sit the *haji saheb*s – senior hijras who have taken a pilgrimage to Mecca (*haj*), and now have returned to live the life of an ascetic and supervise the work of the other hijras. The borders of the *dera*s assigned to each hijra is sacrosanct; any act of transgression, where a *caela* of one guru begins to work in the *dera* of another guru, has the potential to escalate into a full-blown *corcoriya* or turf war that would involve everyone up to the *haji saheb*s themselves.

The gendered manner in which these roles are embodied tells an interesting story about the various conceptions of power that underlie the construction of the hijra society. While guru, *nani*, *dadi* and *gotiya* are typically feminine terms, *caela*, *naek*, *daradin* and *haji* are masculine terms, including the appellation ‘saheb’ that the *haji* is addressed by. This is reflected to an extent in their gender presentation as well. Gurus (who are not *naek*s) usually are castrated, wear sarees, makeup and jewellery, and present themselves in the mould of a local married woman. *Caela*s, who present themselves along very similar aesthetics, are still not considered feminine enough because they are yet to be socialized completely in the ways of the hijras, including their gestures, style of speech and mannerisms. *Naek*s and *hajis*, on the other hand, command a lot of authority, respect and power, so they fashion and present themselves in more masculine ways in terms of their title, body language and voice modulation. *Haji*s are also ascetics, so they typically reject colourful feminine clothes for more pristine, gender-neutral white attire. An intriguing way in which the power relations between a guru and a *caela* find expression is through the custom where some *caela*s choose to wear *sindur* (vermillion put on the forehead, a Hindu symbol of matrimony) in their guru's name, replicating the heterosexual patriarchal model of marriage where the woman wears *sindur* in her husband's name and moves into his house to take care of him, his family and his household.

Here, the guru is cast in the frame of a traditional husband who wields a disproportionate amount of power and control over their *caela* (which is true in case of all guru–*caela* relations), while in their more domestic roles listed previously, the feminine terms and models of kinship are privileged, and the feminine aesthetic and emasculation are valorized. In the latter set of more professional roles, the idea of power is embodied in more conventionally masculine ways. Different ideas of power coalesce and contend with each other in the community to create complex power dynamics which subvert as well as reinforce traditional ideas of power in disparate ways. The gender roles demarcated by mainstream society that has constrained the possibility of self-actualization for the community members for centuries continue to manifest themselves consciously or subconsciously in their interpersonal relationships and social structure, while marking a distinct departure from conventionally heteropatriarchal conceptions of power and masculinity through the figure of the hijra herself.

The hijras in Kalyani and its neighbouring areas like Naihati and Ranaghat were primarily *badhai-ali* (the ones who do *badhai*) until the last decade, who looked down on the other *pesapon* (jobs) typically performed by hijras, like – in decreasing order of prestige – *cholla*/*mangti* (begging in trains, traffic signals, etc.) and *khajra* (sex work). *Logon*, which involved going to the states of Uttar Pradesh (U.P.) and Bihar and dancing in weddings and other events there, had a little more traction. However, with the migration of the youth to other regions for education and jobs and the overall decrease in the rate of childbirth in the region, *badhai* stopped being as lucrative a source of income as it used to be. That is when the *badhai-ali* hijras began to take *cholla-bali* (the ones who do *cholla*) hijras – who earlier used to work within a loosely organized system not intimately connected with the *badhai* system – as their *caela*s to help supplement their income. This is the reason why some *caela*s live away from their gurus: besides the dearth of space in the guru's house, many new *caela*s work in areas which are very far from the guru's house.

While *khajra* remains a frowned-upon occupation in the community because, traditionally, entering the hijra *pratha* (tradition) involved renouncing one's worldly desires and observing celibacy, nowadays many hijras and kotis do engage in *khajra* with or outside the knowledge of their gurus. If discovered, the punishment usually involves paying *don* (fine) to the guru. Similarly, while a few households forbid their *caela*s from having *parik*s or keeping them in the *daiyar*, it has become more common over the years for *caela*s and gurus to have *parik*s. In fact, there is one story where the guru's *giriya*, who had been living in the hijra household with her for years, found the lifestyle so comfortable that he – a cis man – started to wear a saree and perform the hijra identity. He now identifies as a hijra and holds the position of a *naek.* There are also a few cis women in the region who identify as hijras and live within the hijra tradition because they feel safer and more comfortable within this system than outside.

The hijra social framework also contains a quasi-judicial system called *poncit* (panchayat), which comprises a group of *naek*s and senior gurus who act as the jury and preside over any grievance brought before them by a hijra. The matter could be as trivial as a *caela* misbehaving (*biltal kora*) with their guru or stealing something (*bakur kora*) from someone, or as grave as a *corcoraiya* (turf war). The gurus and *naek*s sit on the *poncit*, have a serious discussion regarding the matter (*kalam*), and then decide on a punishment for the offending party, which could be anything from imposing *don* (penalty or fine) on the *caela* to having a guru disown her *caela* and removing her from her household (*thuke deoa*), making the *caela* a *khar golla murod* (a koti without a guru and a *gharana*). In case the *don* is too high for the *caela* to pay (*don*s can run up to lakhs of rupees), she can pawn her jewellery to her guru instead, which is known as giving *citpon*. *Citpon* is also given to be able to accompany a hijra's (who is not one's guru) *badhai* as an ad-hoc member.

As has been discussed in the previous chapter, a majority of hijras are Muslim by faith, so many non-Muslim kotis who join the household often convert to Islam to integrate more seamlessly into the fabric of their guru's lifestyle. Yet, the influence of their home religions permeates every aspect of their existence, making the entire community a confluence of disparate spiritual, religious and ceremonial beliefs and practices that lend a very rich flavour to their lives. Hindu (*changi*) and Muslim (*chulki*) hijras stay in the same household and worship the traditional gods as well as Murugamata (a goddess resembling the four-armed Hindu goddess Amba who is perched on a chicken), who is the patron goddess of the hijra community and is also known as Bahuchara Mata, Bedraj Mata and Maya ji in different parts of the subcontinent (Nanda 1999; Reddy 2005; Hossain 2012). Their reverence for this goddess is also the reason devout hijras abstain from eating chicken. Another important ceremony the hijras perform is *dhol pujo*, which takes place on the day of Kali puja, where the *dhol* (the percussion instrument that is carried to, and played in, *badhais*) is worshipped. An *akhoa murod* (uncastrated man, koti or hijra) is required to perform the ceremony; the next day, the *dhol* is lifted (*dhol othe*) and taken out to *badhai*. It is believed that at least one *badhai* needs to be earned that day as a good omen.

However, when it comes to funerals, hijras reject the religious ceremonies of either religion and perform their own rituals, known as *roti-catai*. After the *shraddha* (Hindu last rites) or the *calisa* (the fortieth day after a hijra's death), her *caela*s go to the homes of other hijras, offer them a symbolic clove (*long deoa*) and invite them to a feast called the *roti* which is arranged in honour of the departed. After the *roti*, a *catai* is convened, which is a meeting where a jury of senior gurus and *naek*s decide how the property and *caela*s of the departed hijra must be divided. If the guru had appointed one of their *caela*s to replace them after their death, then that *caela* gets the guru's *naeki* (*naek*-dom). If not, one of the *caela*s of the guru is selected after great deliberation and appointed the new *naek* of the guru's *birid* ('area'). This ceremony takes place during the *catai* itself, in the presence of the community elders, where the *kundi malik* ('head') anoints the *caela*'s hair with *chameli* oil and drapes them in a white saree (which is smeared with coloured powder in case the *naek* is young, so that they can continue to wear coloured sarees). Thus, a new *naek* inherits their *naeki*.

The ideal of the aspirational feminine beauty is deeply ingrained in the psyche of hijras and kotis, who try to fashion themselves to meet those standards. This attempt is at the heart of the performance of femininity by the community members, as is evidenced by the amount of one's income that is spent on buying the best makeup, accessories and clothes one can afford. The idea of feminine *shringaar* (adornment) is held sacred by the community, many of whom find the sight of a biologically male person sporting a beard while wearing a saree and makeup repulsive. This sentiment probably stems from the underlying anxiety that if the culturally fixed notions of femininity are diluted or subverted in the public forum, the community members may be under threat of violence for ostensibly being 'fake' hijras and 'converting' the young men of the area into hijras as well. This manifests in the form of aggression directed at kotis or other persons on social media who bend and blend the neat, dichotomous conceptions of gendered aesthetics in their personal gender presentation.

In the words of Aniruddha Dutta, who has worked extensively with the community over the last decade, the community itself is going through a transitional phase and has been in constant flux over the last few years, resulting in a turbulent, ever-shifting system that is 'messy and rigid at the same time' (interview with Dutta, 2020). In other words, anything that might be considered a convention today and that is implemented firmly could very well be unacceptable tomorrow.

In such a scenario, where gurus and *caela*s are constantly shifting allegiances, and customs and categories of identity are ambiguous at best, it is likely that some of the descriptions and definitions I have presented in this chapter may not be accurate in a few years' time, but they are faithful to the realities of the community as it stands today.

## Conclusion

The theme of gender, and particularly femininity, lies at the heart of the hijra-koti experience. From their names to gender identities to gender presentation, appearance and behaviour, to their romantic and kinship relations as members of the community, their lives are spent expanding and re-negotiating the terms of femininity and trying to situate their own subjectivities in relation to various mainstream and community-internal constructions of femininit(ies). Thus we see in the community a wide range of gender expressions and ideas about what constitutes femininity and the ideal hijra or koti figure, from conservative attitudes that aspire to traditional standards of feminine aesthetics, submissiveness and domesticity, to more modern, cosmopolitan and transnational expressions of gender identity that do not consider gender-ambiguous or 'masculine' names, bodies or attires to be necessarily at odds with the image and identity of the 'feminine' or femme associated with hijras and kotis. While the act of castration has historically been central to the conceptualization of the hijra figure and remains a major part of the hijra identity construction till date, it is no longer unusual to hear of hijras who still bear penises. Meanwhile, many kotis undergo sex reassignment surgeries, and many others find themselves unable or unwilling to do so for various reasons – financial, psychological and personal. They all constitute active and involved members of the community. There are no clear lines that demarcate between hijra and koti bodies any more; in fact, the centrality of the body and its transformation in the construction of the hijra and koti subject is increasingly being rejected by the community itself, who instead argue for the validity of their identities based on psychological and emotional identification with their gender alone.

In such sociocultural contexts, we do not see an environment where community participation and the use of the hijra-koti language is governed and mediated by one's bodily transformation – whether surgically or in terms of attire and aesthetic expression, as Borba and Ostermann (2007) seem to suggest. Following their research on code-switching patterns in Brazilian Portuguese, they suggest that:

> In order to deepen understandings of the links between gender and language use (especially in the case of transgenderism) researchers should bear in mind how language users embody local understandings of gender and sexuality onto their bodies and this embodiment enables users to frame their language use accordingly to surrounding ideologies about gendered and sexual beings. *Transgender language should be taken as a result of the gendered meanings (re)constructed through body practices.* As the body is the main medium through which transgenders assert their identities in the intersection of socially available genders, it must be understood as a catalyst for discourses of masculinity and femininity. Thus, it is *upon (re)signifying their bodies that transgendered people have privileged access to a multitude of identity positions which is partly conveyed in the ways they use language to place themselves between the boundaries of the gender dichotomy.* Needless to say, gendered bodily meanings are context-based, varying greatly from one culture to another. (Ibid.: 144; emphases added)

The authors developed this theory, in part, after reading Hall and O'Donovan's (1996) work on the code-switching patterns of the Hindi-speaking hijras of Delhi who, like the *travesti*s of Brazilian-Portuguese, switch their grammatical gender agreement to index their masculine and feminine identities respectively. Zimman and Hall (2010) agree with and expand Borba and Ostermann's theory that transgender languages are embodied because:

> [T]he examples taken from [their] research among transsexual men and hijras suggest a discursive relationship between language and embodiment. On the one hand, language shapes our understanding of the human body and its meanings. . . . On the other, language is also an embodied undertaking in that it collaborates with gesture as part of a broader communicative act. In the hijra community, the deployment of the flat-palmed claps marks the hijras as external to the normative gender binary. For the hijras who offer fertility blessings and the kotis who parody them, gesture helps to accomplish identity work, even distinguishing a self-identified 'third sex' from their 'fourth breed' imitators. (Ibid.: 177–78)

These arguments are problematic on many counts. While it is true that our understanding of gender roles and identities are constructed and resignified through language, it is a discursive process that occurs in every language to a certain extent; it is not something that is specific and unique to hijra or transgender languages. It is also important to note that since Ulti shows no gender agreement or gendered code-switching patterns akin to Brazilian-Portuguese and Hindi, it cannot be conceived of as embodied in the way these languages have been. While Ulti speakers do embody a spectrum of overlapping yet distinct gender identities, the language does not capture most of that diversity in either its lexical items or its grammatical structure. Further, not every Ulti speaker necessarily 'resignifies their bodies' to perform femininity, nor is it imperative that their patterns of use of Ulti be in direct correlation with any process of bodily transformation.

Moreover, to associate hijra languages with extralinguistic signifiers of hijra identity like gestures and claps (which have not been explored in this book precisely because they are extralinguistic features and outside the purview of this research), and argue that this is one of the ways hijra languages are embodied and hijra identity performed, is a very limited way of understanding the role and significance of such languages. Hijra languages do not merely exist to 'accomplish identity work', but are a means of ensuring the personal security of its speakers in public spaces and forging bonds of camaraderie and kinship within the community.

Further, as mentioned above, its use is not dependent on the bodily form or gendered appearance of its speakers, whether it is in online or offline mode. To think of such languages as embodied is biologically essentialist and relocates the body at the centre of the conversation on transgenderism, which is reductive and does not take into account the spectrum of identities that constitute the hijra and koti community. This multiplicity of identities is not acknowledged by Hall, whose characterization of hijras and kotis as 'third gender' and 'fourth breed' along a schemata is rigid and not reflective of the wide-ranging fluidity, overlap and ambiguity between the two categories that renders any such schematization redundant and incapable of being translated across the various regions and sociocultural contexts in which hijras and kotis exist within the subcontinent.

## Notes

[1] This was a panel discussion streamed on Facebook on 2 August 2020. The panelists were Ani Dutta, Sumi Das and A.R. Chowdhuri. Reproduced here with permission, available at https://www.facebook.com/aniruddha.dutta1/videos/1015847499465738 3?idorvanity=100004471295431, accessed 14 April 2023.

[2] Dutta (2022: 2) defines *lagan*, also known as *launda nac,* as 'a performative practice

where feminine boys or trans people known as *launda*s or *laganvali*s, many of whom are migrants from West Bengal, dance in socially designated female attire at weddings and socioreligious festivals in parts of northern India such as eastern Uttar Pradesh and western Bihar (Dasgupta 2013; Morcom 2013)'.

3 International Symposium on Trans Community/Spectrum of the South Asian Diaspora, 'Amalgamation of Academia and Activism', organized by Indian Queers' Collective, 18 December 2020.

4 *Badhai*: blessing new-borns and newly-weds in exchange for gifts in cash and kind.

5 *Cholla*: begging, usually in trains and traffic signals.

6 *Khajra*: sex work.

7 Neel Naach: A seven-day Bacchanalian festival organized by kotis and cismen that takes place in the second week of April, leading up to the Bengali new year's day, or *Poila Boisakh*. Here, kotis, hijras and others dress up as men and women, dance and enact roles of gods and goddesses on stage, take a *giriya* (lover) for those seven days, roam around the town, and essentially celebrate and enjoy themselves to the brim. This festival is known to be the place to go if one wants to meet a lot of kotis together. New kotis are usually brought here to be introduced to the larger community for the first time.

8 It is noteworthy that there also exist a few hijras who strongly identify as hijras outside of the guru–*caela* system and are not affiliated to any *gharana*. However, they are the exception; most hijras consider the guru–*caela* system to be the most legitimate way of defining the hijra identity and, by extension, structuring the hijra community (Dutta 2012).

# 3

# Speaking Ulti

## A Lexical Analysis

In this chapter, we look at the selection of lexical items in Ulti and the domains in which they occur, and analyse how their occurrence and patterns of usage are influenced by the sociocultural context(s) in which hijras and kotis lead their lives. In the first section, we reflect on the need to document minority languages, the ethical and practical conundrums we are faced with when the language is secret, like Ulti, and how we can work around those issues. In the second section, we discuss the concept of semantic domains and then go on to analyse the domains Ulti is spoken in, the variety of lexical items in those domains and the significance of those domains vis-à-vis the lives of the hijra-koti community. We also examine the grammatical categories and the phonological, semantic and syntactic properties of the words present in Ulti, and compare selected lexical items from the few hijralects hitherto documented in the Indian subcontinent to establish the existence of etymological and cross-linguistic connections between them.

### Lexicography and the Problem of Ulti

One of the fundamental components of the linguistic study of any language is the process of collecting, compiling and analysing data. Most major, well-documented languages have enough corpora and scholarly literature on the language, besides easy access to native speakers, that enables researchers to explore theoretical questions about and conduct experiments on the language without needing to document the language from the basics. The story, however, is different in the case of unwritten languages.

The process of documenting unwritten, undocumented languages typically starts with the collection of a basic list of words and sentences, which are then analysed at the lexical, phonological, morphological, syntactic, semantic and pragmatic levels in an attempt to study and understand the rules governing the grammar of those languages. In the case of a language like Ulti, which is not only unwritten but also secret and comprises of a specialized, domain-restricted lexicon spoken by a community of oppressed, marginalized people, the process of data collection becomes similarly specialized, presenting the researcher with ethical and practical questions that they might not have to consider while working on other minority or unwritten languages.

The critical questions we need to ask are:

(1) Why are we interested in documenting Ulti?
(2) How does the special status of Ulti inform the method of data collection in the language?

In our logocentric epistemological culture, the act of documenting a language is a consequence of the human conceit that it can be thus preserved for eternity, much like the mummy embalmed and enshrined within a museum, divorced from its cultural and functional contexts. Living languages evolve with time; documenting them is tantamount to keeping a synchronic snapshot of a language as it was spoken at a certain time and place, to be studied by present and future scholars.

However, when it comes to endangered or nearly extinct languages, this act of documentation becomes an urgent attempt to preserve the grammatical, cultural and civilizational knowledge encoded in the language before the last of its speakers die out[1] and it is erased by an encroaching majority language. In other words, despite the inherent problematics of the act of documenting an oral language, it becomes the final means of recording the words, grammar and sounds of a language that is rapidly losing its vitality within its speech community. Documenting a language becomes a means of preserving an essential part of the identity, culture and knowledge system of a community, and can subsequently be used to retain and revitalize[2] the language by reintroducing it to its speech community as a prestigious and viable language in their altered sociocultural contexts. One of the ways to achieve this is to develop primers and textbooks in that language, to compile dictionaries that will help people learn the language, and to generally share the language with the world.

Ulti, however, is a different story. It exists in the shadows of mainstream society, spoken by a marginalized community whose survival, in many contexts, depends upon the fact that knowledge of Ulti's very existence is hidden from those who wield the power to abuse, exploit and oppress them. It is not a language its speakers would be keen on sharing with the world, unlike speakers of other minority languages, especially as it would directly impact the speakers' ability to practise their professions with relative security and ease in public spaces.

The ethical conundrum of my role as a researcher in 'exposing' their language to the public while attempting to study its unique features has weighed on me since the inception of this study, which was further complicated by the community's stance on the subject. On the one hand, the primary participants in this research work – bemused by my interest in their language yet eager to help me out – reassured me that my work would not compromise the safety of the community because the language is not as strictly secret in the region as it used to be. A few Ulti words and phrases have featured in books and songs in the recent past, and some hijras and kotis have introduced a few popular Ulti words to their friends and allies, who would occasionally use them in conversation. However, they also cautioned me against mentioning the subject of my research to any community member unless encouraged by them to do so, fearing a backlash from them rooted in anxiety regarding their collective safety and security, and stemming from complicated interpersonal dynamics within the community.

The motivation to document Ulti, meanwhile, is more academically oriented than community-oriented. It is a language that has emerged from similar kinds of secret languages that have thrived across the subcontinent for centuries, but have escaped detection and documentation until recently. The lack of information on what these languages may have looked like initially, how they may have evolved and how they may have been used constitutes a major gap in the literature, which has consequently hampered our understanding of the community and contributed to their continued marginalization and segregation from mainstream spaces. This is not to argue that the community is obligated to share information about themselves with the mainstream academic community for the latter's intellectual benefit – quite the opposite. The community stands to gain practically nothing from sharing such privileged information.

This brings us to the practical conundrum. The ideal solution from the vantage point of the hijra-koti community, short of abandoning the study altogether, would be to find a way to document and analyse the language without advertising its contents to the whole world. The key to accomplishing that would be to do the former but refrain from publishing the findings – a self-defeating goal. The second-best solution would be to publish only as much of the language as is necessary to gain an understanding of its grammar and its role and significance within the community, steering clear of constructions that would put the community in any immediate danger. That precludes the end to which much research in unwritten minority languages is geared towards: the development of a dictionary and/or a primer in the language under study.

Incidentally, that leaves us at an advantage. The process of documenting, describing and developing a dictionary and an orthography for an oral language invariably involves a process of standardization, neglecting the rich variations within the language and 'fixing' one variety as the documented standard – the prestige variety – to be learned and adhered to by the subsequent generations. But the absence of an Ulti dictionary has the advantage of not privileging one variety of Ulti over the others; thus the linguistic diversity of Ulti and its regional varieties within Bengal is retained. This book describes only one of those varieties – the one with standard Bangla as its ML (matrix language), because standard Bangla is the lingua franca of the region, making this variety of Ulti the most commonly spoken one – while recognizing the other varieties as equally interesting and worthy of future research.

Secret languages like Ulti have been documented on a few occasions, the most famous of which are the Cant dictionaries published in Great Britain in the eighteenth century. These dictionaries, compiled by Captain Grose, among others, documented nearly 4,000 entries from Cant (a secret criminal language that, like Ulti, was 'consciously invented' and 'clearly gendered') and other non-standard languages spoken by the 'vulgar' or lower-class populace of Britain (Sorensen 2004; Baker 2019). The very act of documenting these linguistic varieties through a process of practical lexicography, in this case, reclaimed and legitimized the 'substandard expressions' and linguistic forms that were earlier devalued during the compilation of the English language dictionaries, and 'reconfigure[d] the languages of putative outsiders as signs of British national culture, incorporating the people into the rhetorical space of the nation via those linguistic practices' (Sorensen 2004: 435). In other words, the very act of documentation has the power to legitimize the identity and culture of the speakers of a language, and include them as part of the national imagination and conversation.

However, this process also led to the erasure and elision of some other rural folk and non-standard varieties, which were subsumed under the broader rubric of Cant, thereby 'isolat[ing] . . . non-standard language[s] as a curious object of amusement', and 'relegat[ing] the people, imputed inventors and users of vulgar language, to [a] past . . . emptied of specific labour histories, bereft of the material connections of canting crews to labouring classes, and amnesic of the shared working lives of men and women'(ibid.: 449). This potential of practical lexicography to dehistoricize and decontextualize a language and its speech community, and erase or obfuscate its concurrent varieties from archival memory through the mere act of selecting this one variety for documentation, is the eventuality that this book seeks to avoid by foregoing the attempt to build a formal dictionary of the language.

In its stead, we will focus on theoretical lexicography in this chapter, which has been broadly defined as 'a body of theory related to lexicography' (Atkins 1992: 4), or, more specifically, as 'the scholarly discipline of analysing and describing the semantic, syntagmatic and paradigmatic relationships within the lexicon of a language'.[3] Atkins goes on to discuss the need for lexicographers to learn from theoretical linguists (such as sociolinguists, psycholinguists, experts in stylistics and textual analysis) the 'structured approach to the lexical entry and its contents, their theory-based insights into word meaning, and their rigorous factoring out of word sense relationships' (ibid.: 30), in order to resolve some of the recurring problems practical lexicographers encounter in the process of dictionary-making. This chapter aims to present analyses and insights of this nature that I have arrived at as a result of collecting and analysing the lexical items of Ulti.

To answer, then, the first question posed at the beginning of the section, we are interested in documenting Ulti because it presents us with a set of lexical items, constrained by domains of use, that are unique to the language (and its regional counterparts), and offers us the chance to explore the semantic relations between them and examine the reasons behind the coinage of those specific lexical items in the language. Further, from a diachronic perspective, it is invaluable to document any language to enable future researchers to study the phonological, morphological, lexical, semantic and grammatical changes, if any, that may have taken place in the language over time. In Hone, an African language, it has been observed that a set of conscious morphological manipulations (transposition from prefix to suffix) made by the speakers to create marked forms in a special register (that would make it obscure and difficult to identify for the speakers of the corresponding mainstream language), has now become a part of modern Hone (Storch 2011).

In the case of Ulti, any such structural changes – besides posing interesting theoretical questions about the transitory nature of secret languages, and what, specifically, are the forms and constructions that make a language 'secret' from their surrounding languages – would also engender questions about the changes in the socioeconomic conditions, self-perception and occupational patterns of the speech community over the years; the evolution of the sociocultural role of the community and the language in relation to mainstream communities and languages; whether the in-community status and nature of secrecy of the language has altered in any way; and whether such sociological factors or ideological shifts can have and have had any bearing on the observable structural or lexical changes that may have occurred in the language.

## Semantic Domains

The process of data collection in Ulti was contingent on its special role within the larger linguistic repertoire of its speakers, and this was most explicitly revealed while collecting Ulti lexical data using the Dictionary Development Programme (DDP) method developed by Ronald Moe of SIL (Summer Institute of Linguistics) International. It is a highly productive method that enables the linguist to collect around 9,000–12,000 words in two weeks using the concept of semantic domains (Moe 2003; van den Berg and Shore 2006).

> The concept of Semantic Domains . . . is inspired by the 'Theory of Semantic Fields' a structural model for lexical semantics proposed by Jost Trier at the beginning of the last century. The basic assumption is that the lexicon is structured into Semantic Fields: semantic relations among concepts belonging to the same field are very dense, while concepts belonging to different fields are typically unrelated. . . . Semantic Domains are clusters of terms and texts that exhibit a high level of lexical coherence, i.e., the property of domain-specific words to co-occur together in texts. . . . Semantic Domains correspond to both lexical fields and conceptual fields. (Gliozzo and Strapparava 2009: 13)

Gliozzo and Strapparava (2009) further add that semantic domains correspond to both lexical fields and conceptual fields. As a result of the advanced level of lexical coherence in the minds of the speakers of a language, it has been observed that when words from a specific domain are elicited, other words from that domain that have strong lexical relations and mental associations with them quickly follow, making the process of data collection a very quick and systematic one. Moe (2003) has developed a set of questions and examples based on 1,700 semantic domains, known as the Rapid Word Collection (RWC) method, which is designed to prompt the speaker to think of words related to the ones being elicited. For instance, in the domain of 'physical universe', the linguist would elicit words for certain universal words such as sky, water, soil, etc., and then ask questions like 'what grows in the soil', 'what lives in the water' and so on, to elicit as many lexical items for flora and fauna as are available in the language in a short span of time. This list of domains and examples, while elaborate, is not exhaustive; it would require modifications depending on the cultural and environmental contexts specific to the speech community of the language being documented, so as to efficiently elicit the range of lexical items in use in every domain that the language has to offer.

### *Ulti Domains*

The domains in which Ulti is used are specific – and, in certain cases, exclusive – to the hijra community and experience, with words pertaining to hijra social structures, kinship terms, rituals, customs, occupations, finance, bodies, beauty and aesthetics, sexual acts, gender identities and medical terminology. Words pertaining to any other domain, like education (which hijras were kept away from for generations), or agriculture, topography, weather, trade, popular culture, etc., that have not been silenced or made taboo in mainstream culture, do not feature in the set of bare Ulti lexical items. In other words, the figure of the hijra and the social organization of the hijra subculture have been at the epicentre of the development of languages like Ulti, which have flourished as a result of the need to respond to the silences imposed by dominant languages and cultures and coin words to construct and organize a subculture that would become a safe, liberating and familial space for the socially marginalized community of hijras to live and thrive in.

Predictably, some of these domains (hijra social structure, hijra customs and rituals) have not been listed by Moe, as well as some others that are specific to Indian cultures (like kinship terms, beauty and aesthetics, and so on). As a result, the Ulti lexical data was collected using two data elicitation tools – the RWC method, and the word list and sentence list compiled and developed by Anvita Abbi (2001) from Swadesh's (1955) and Gudschinsky's (1956) lists.

The RWC was used first to elicit words from different domains. At the beginning of the research, when it was unclear how many domains Ulti was used in, I tried to follow the questionnaire developed by Moe quite diligently. But it soon became clear that in the absence of many domains in which Ulti was not used, like topography, repeated questions of a similar nature, which were asked in my attempt to ensure no possible lexical item was missed, was beginning to annoy the participants. For instance, if I had been told that there is no word for 'mountain', then to ask if there was a word for 'beach' or 'sea' or 'desert' in Ulti (there wasn't) was likely to elicit an impatient response. I had to maintain a balance between being meticulous and holding my participants' interest in my questions, which is when I began to treat the questionnaire more as a document to refer to than one to be followed. I followed the RWC technique to elicit words from domains I was sure they had, like the domains of gender identity and sexual activity, which restored their interest and enthusiasm in the discussion and helped me elicit a wide variety of lexical items (and sentences they can be used in) from those domains as well as other, related domains.

Around this time my participants reiterated a few times the fact that Ulti only contained words that the hijras and kotis wanted to hide from – or were not allowed to use by – the mainstream society. To hear them describe these, it would seem the semantic domains in Ulti and Bangla were mutually exclusive. However, I soon discovered that there were domains in the two languages that overlapped with each other, though with distinct lexical items, like the domains of food, addictive substances and biological kinship terms. It appeared that the range of Ulti lexical items spanned certain concepts that are relevant to the life of a hijra or koti, even if they are not necessarily taboo subjects, like the words for 'river' (*gaŋ mashi*), 'water' (*pani mashi*), 'mirror' (*shisha mashi/dorpon mashi*), 'house' (*khol*), etc.

Once the RWC method had been exhaustively employed (after checking for all possible kinds of domains), I used Abbi's (2001) word list and sentence list to double-check if I had missed something. The word list had largely been covered with the help of the RWC method (with many blank spaces beside words that had no Ulti counterpart), but the use of the translation method ensured that certain words, like the ones for 'dog' (*gheugheu mashi*), 'snake' (*snek mashi*) or 'river' (*gaang mashi*), which had previously been missed out, were elicited now. It is essential to note that in Ulti, these are all rare exceptions in the domains of wildlife and topography, respectively. These domains barely have two or three lexical items (the lexical items for fauna include individual words for different species like dog, snake and housefly) with weak lexical relations amongst them, which is why the concept of lexical coherence does not work here as an effective means of eliciting all these words through the RWC method. The translation method, however, has severe limitations, which is why it could not be used exclusively to elicit lexical data in Ulti.

The sentence list was also elicited using the translation method, which posed some unique challenges. Even though the Ulti grammar is very close to the Bangla grammar, many sentences that were meant to elicit grammatical information about the language would elicit no response because the questions were asked in the contact language, Bangla, and the content words in those sentences had no Ulti counterparts, which meant that the response would be the same as the question, i.e. the same Bangla sentence. In order to work around this, I would modify or sometimes change the sentences to include words that I knew had Ulti counterparts, taking care to adhere to the grammatical structure of the question, in order to elicit an Ulti sentence and analyse whether or not it had the same structure as its Bangla counterpart. The translation method also poses a challenge while eliciting sentential data because, often, the participants alter the sentence in response such that the content remains the same but not the form. In such cases, it becomes essential to modify the question and instruct the participants in various ways – sometimes by demonstrating an example, sometimes by prompting a specific response, and sometimes by explaining exactly what structure one is looking for – so that we might be able to elicit the required sentence.

The techniques described above have been instrumental in eliciting most of the lexical and sentential data in Ulti, which was further supplemented by lexical items that the participants would hear used in various conversations within the community, note them down and share with me in our next meeting. The same technique was adopted in reverse, where upon coming across any Ulti word I was not familiar with on social media or in casual discussions or the discourses recorded by me for my research, I would take them to my participants and request them to tell me the meanings of those words and how they could be used in a sentence.

An analysis of the lexical items of Ulti illustrates how they are chosen for a sociolect that has developed for specific purposes and is used in a few, select domains. The following data have been sorted by semantic domains and present the Ulti lexical item, its Bangla counterpart (if any), the meaning of the lexical item as used in Ulti and the grammatical category of the lexical item.

*Semantic Domain: Sexual and Gender Identities and Presentation*

This domain contains the terminology for gender and sexual identities recognized by this speech community, as well as terms for certain kinds of gender presentation. Here, we see that it is primarily the lexical items for identities in the hijra-koti spectrum that Bangla has no counterpart for. Even the word 'hijra' has emerged from the hijra community. For cisgender identities, especially heteronormative ones like man and woman, Bangla has many lexical counterparts. The word for homosexual is a recent addition in the Bangla lexicon, and is a calque or loan translation of the English word 'homosexual'. The words that describe types of masculinity also have counterparts in Bangla, and are mostly used (in Bangla) to pass value judgements on a person assigned male at birth based on how they present and perform their masculinities.

**Table 3.1** ***Sexual and gender identities and presentation***

| No. | Ulti lexical item | Bangla counterpart | Meaning | Grammatical category |
|---|---|---|---|---|
| 1 | gʊpt̪i kot̪i | – | koti who is closeted; presents like a man | N |
| 2 | bʰelki/bʰɔrokt̪i kot̪i | – | koti who is out; presents like a woman with saree, lots of make-up, jewellery | N |
| 3 | bʰel kɔra | – | to perform femininity (being seductive, coquettish, flamboyant, etc.)<br>there is a sense of pleasure, achievement, agency and pride in the artifice inherent in *bhel kora* | V |
| 4 | bʰɔbraʃi | – | intersex person | N |
| 5 | cʰibri | hiɟra | hijra | N |
| 6 | ɖubli/ɖəbəl-ɖekər | – | someone who takes on both dominant and submissive roles in a sexual relationship | N |
| 7 | t̪onna | puruʃ/cʰele | cisgender man | N |
| 8 | laharan/niharini | mohila/meje | cisgender woman | N |
| 9 | raɟa pont̪ʰi/lebu | ʃɔmokami (formal) | lesbian (lit: like man) | N |
| 10 | mouga/maiga | mouga/ maiga/ mejeli | effeminate man; one who dresses up like a woman | N |
| 11 | mɔrd̪a | puruʃali (adj) | masculine man | N |

*Semantic Domain: Body Parts*

One of the most important domains where Ulti is used is the human body and the many things associated with it, like adornments, sexual organs, sexual activities, sex reassignment surgery and so on. The lexical items for body parts clearly illustrate one of the main reasons for the genesis of a language like Ulti. Ulti contains lexical items for body parts that are considered inappropriate to mention in 'polite' circles, like primary and secondary sexual organs (and the bodily and sexual activities associated with them), as well as body parts that are culturally considered to be markers of beauty, aesthetics and femininity, like eyes, teeth, face, mouth and hair. Lexical items for body parts like arms,

**Table 3.2** ***Body parts***

| No. | Ulti lexical item | Bangla counterpart | Meaning | Grammatical category |
|---|---|---|---|---|
| 12 | ɟog | cul | hair | N |
| 13 | ɑ$^{n}$k$^{h}$ijɑ mɑʃi | cok$^{h}$ | eyes | N |
| 14 | d̪ont̪o mɑʃi | d̪ɑ$^{n}$t̪ | teeth | N |
| 15 | k$^{h}$umur | muk$^{h}$ | face/mouth | N |
| 16 | d̪ɔrʃon | lom/cimt̪ɑ | body hair/razor | N |
| 17 | likɔm | liŋgo (formal) | penis | N |
| 18 | cipt̪i | ɟoni (archaic) | vagina | N |
| 19 | bɑt̪t̪u | pɑc$^{h}$ɑ | buttocks | N |
| 20 | bɑt̪li | pod̪ | anus | N |
| 21 | d̪$^{h}$ɑrki | bu:k | breasts | N |
| 22 | mɔd̪on rɔʃ | – | semen | N |
| 23 | c$^{h}$ibri | – | site of the unhealed castration injury | N |

shoulders, knees and legs do not exist in Ulti, because they are neither taboo words nor carry a special significance in the lives of the community members.

Ulti also contains lexical items for bodily functions like 'urinating' (*sudhrano*), 'farting' (*potka/thushki camano*), 'excreting' (*pakki kora*) and 'ejaculating' (*jhinni potano*) because their Bangla counterparts are considered dirty or taboo, and conversations around them – especially ejaculation – are to a large extent silenced in dominant discursive spaces.

While there are words for sexual organs in Bangla, those are either formal, archaic words which are not used in everyday speech, or 'slang' words which have several negative, vulgar connotations attached to them that the hijra-koti community do not like to use to describe their existing and aspirational bodies. Ulti also contains an LI for the part of the body that has recently been castrated and is healing which has no Bangla counterpart, because this is an experience that is unique to the hijra community.

*Semantic Domain: Sexual Acts*

The sexual organs that have Ulti lexical items also have corresponding verbal forms that describe the sexual act pertaining to them (see Table 3.3). Ulti contains the above words as well as words for (male) partners and lovers, but no words for love, as that is not a taboo sentiment and can be expressed in

**Table 3.3** ***Sexual acts***

| No. | Ulti lexical item | Bangla counterpart | Meaning | Grammatical category |
|---|---|---|---|---|
| 24 | d̪ʰurano/d̪ʰurpit̪t̪i kɔra | – | to have sex | V |
| 25 | cipt̪i d̪ʰurano | – | to have vaginal sex | V |
| 26 | likɔm kʰumur kɔra | – | to give a blowjob | V |
| 27 | hat̪ʰ maʃi kora | – | to masturbate/give a handjob | V |
| 28 | bat̪t̪u dʰurano | – | to have anal sex | V |
| 29 | bat̪li uŋgli kɔra | – | to finger the anus | V |
| 30 | d̪ʰarki t̪aka | – | to suck the nipples | V |
| 31 | camacami kɔra | – | to flirt or seduce | V |

Bangla in public without anyone raising their eyebrows or easily detecting if the love being alluded to is of a non-conventional kind.

In the domain of medicine, lexical items alluding to the process of sex reassignment surgery are usually borrowed from English, like hormone therapy, counselling, etc. However, the essential processes that mark pivotal stages in one's journey of transitioning, like 'castration' (*chibrano*) and 'vaginal construction' (*cipti kora*), can be expressed in Ulti. As has been mentioned before, *chibrano* is an especially central term in the language because the endonym for hijra, i.e. *chibri*, comes from the same root, indicating the pivotal role of the ritual of penectomy within the hijra tradition to mark the transition of a *dhurani* or a koti into a *chhibri* or a hijra.

### *Semantic Domain: Accessories and Adornments*

The performance of femininity is an important part of the hijra-koti identity and culture. This is achieved by pursuing the standards of beauty and femininity for cisgender women that have currency at any given time and place, most of which involve makeup, jewellery, long hair and feminine clothes. The face and hair – which are amongst the few non-sexual body parts to have Ulti lexical items – are the sites on which the items of makeup and hair accessories listed below are used. This results in high lexical coherence between the two sets of lexical items, and explains their existence and significance in the language.

The items *ʃad̪a maʃi* and *lali maʃi*, in Table 3.4, do not refer only to lipstick and face powder. They have a variety of senses that vary with context; literally, they mean 'the white thing' and 'the red thing', respectively, and can be used to

**Table 3.4** ***Accessories and adornments***

| No. | Ulti lexical item | Bangla counterpart | Meaning | Grammatical category |
|---|---|---|---|---|
| 31 | ilu-ilu | – | fake breast made up of balloons (worn under a padded bra) | N |
| 32 | kɔʈora | – | padding to put inside padded bra to make a fake breast | |
| 33 | lali maʃi | – | lipstick | N |
| 34 | ʃad̪a maʃi | – | face powder | N |
| 35 | ʈʰɔʃʃok | – | makeup | N |
| 36 | kʰauri ɟog | fɔls cul | wig | N |
| 37 | ʃat̪ra | ʃaɽi/kapoɽ | saree/clothes | N |
| 38 | pilka | ʃona | gold | N |
| 39 | ɟʰorni | gɔjna | jewellery | N |
| 40 | d̪ʰonnu maʃi | kaner d̪ul | earrings | N |

refer to anything associated with the colours white or red. For instance, a common meaning of *lali maʃi* is menstruation, 'red' referring to menstrual blood. This indicates that not all Ulti words have been coined to speak exclusively about the experiences of the hijra-koti community. As the compound for pregnancy (*kʰol pakki*, lit. 'the house is full') also indicates, Ulti is likely to have an LI for any bodily function that is taboo in mainstream discourse – not spoken of often or openly in the public domain.

### *Semantic Domain: Biological Kinship Terms*

Kinship terms in Ulti are of two kinds: those pertaining to one's biological family and those pertaining to one's hijra family. Table 3.5 illustrates the biological kinship terms, all of which have Bangla counterparts as these are all normative relationships.

Barring the gender-neutral word for sibling, every other kinship term in the table above is binary-gendered. It is significant that there are no kinship terms for marital relationships and in-laws in Ulti, even though the word for 'wedding' (*chiya*) exists in the lexicon. There is no word for bride or wife either, but there is one for a 'husband' or 'long-term lover' (*girija*). This illustrates the centrality of the hijra-koti figure behind the conceptualization of the language itself: lexical items only for those concepts or people exist

**Table 3.5** ***Biological kinship terms***

| No. | Ulti lexical item | Bangla counterpart | Meaning | Grammatical category |
|---|---|---|---|---|
| 41 | sʊɖɖʰɑ | bɑbɑ/buʈo | father/old man | N |
| 42 | sʊɖɖʰi | mɑ/buʈi | mother/old woman | N |
| 43 | piʈ mɑʃi | – | sibling | N |
| 44 | piʈ tonnɑ | bʰɑi | brother | N |
| 45 | piʈ lɑhɑrɑn/ʈunni | Bon | sister | N |
| 46 | bɔʈkɑ piʈ | d̪ɑd̪ɑ/d̪id̪i | elder sibling | N |
| 47 | cʰoʈkɑ piʈ | (cʰoʈo) bʰɑi/bon | younger sibling | N |
| 48 | sʊɖɖʰir piʈ | mɑmɑ/mɑʃi | mother's sibling | N |
| 49 | ʈæpkɑ | cʰele | young boy | N |
| 50 | ʈepki | meje | young girl | N |

that have a direct impact or connection with the lives of the speakers. They are used to being abandoned by their cis male lovers who go on to marry cis women, but rarely find themselves in the role of a bride or a wife, which makes the existence of marital kinship terms irrelevant to their lives.

*Semantic Domain: Hijra Kinship Terms*

The hijra *gharana* acts as a surrogate, chosen family unit with very rigid hierarchies, where the guru is addressed as *ma* ('mother') by the *cæla*, who is referred to as 'daughter'. The guru of the guru is the *nanguru*, who is addressed as *nani* ('mother's mother') by the *caela*, and the guru of the *nanguru* is the *d̪ad̪guru* or *d̪ad̪i* ('father's mother'). The *caela* of one's *caela* becomes the *nat̪i cæla* ('grand-*caela* [M]'), while one's co-*caela* under the same guru is one's *got̪ija* ('sister'), and one's guru's *got̪ija* becomes one's *kʰalija guru* ('mother's sister'). None of these lexical items have Bangla counterparts, as these are relations and dynamics exclusive to the hijra *gharana*s.

The koti identity is defined in relation to the figure of (and in response to their desire for) a *parik*, *pont̪ʰi* or *girija* – a cis male lover. They are seminal figures in the lives of kotis and hijras, which makes the presence of lexical items for them, and distinguishing between short-term and long-term lovers, inevitable. These relationships are modelled on those of cisgender heterosexual couples (married or dating) romanticized in popular culture, which is why, despite having separate Ulti terms for them, the English term 'boyfriend' or Bangla term *bɔr* ('husband') are also sometimes used to refer to these persons.

**Table 3.6** ***Hijra kinship terms***

| No. | Ulti lexical item | Bangla counterpart | Meaning | Grammatical category |
|---|---|---|---|---|
| 51 | guru /mɑ | – | guru | N |
| 52 | cælɑ | – | disciple | N |
| 53 | nɑnguru/nɑni | – | guru of guru | N |
| 54 | d̪ɑdguru/d̪ɑd̪i | – | guru of *nanguru* | N |
| 55 | got̪ijɑ | bon | co-disciple under a guru/sister | N |
| 56 | kʰɑlijɑ guru | – | *gotija* of guru | N |
| 57 | nɑt̪i cælɑ | – | *caela* of *caela* | N |
| 58 | pɑrik | premik/bond̪ʰu | cis male lover/ boyfriend (usually short-term) | N |
| 59 | girijɑ/pont̪ʰi | premik/bond̪ʰu | cis male lover/ husband (long- term) | N |

*Semantic Domain: Hierarchy Terms*

Besides the hijra kinship terms, a few other terms exist in the hijra social system to refer to figures who exist in relation to each other in a rigid hierarchy of power, and the areas and people they have command over. While Bangla words exist for different kinds of areas where hijras work, they, predictably, do not exist for the hijra gurus who run them.

**Table 3.7** ***Hierarchy terms***

| No. | Ulti lexical item | Bangla counterpart | Meaning | Grammatical category |
|---|---|---|---|---|
| 60 | pɑrɑ birid̪ | pɑrɑ | neighbourhood | N |
| 61 | ɖerɑ | elɑkɑ | a collection of *para birids* | N |
| 62 | d̪ɑrɑd̪in | – | head of a *dera* | N |
| 63 | nɑek | – | head of a collection of *dera*s | N |
| 64 | birid̪ | elɑkɑ | area comprising 2–3 towns; has a bunch of *naek*s working in it | N |
| 65 | kunɖi | – | senior *naek*, head of a *birid*, adjudicator of disputes | N |
| 66 | hɑɟi ʃɑheb | – | senior hijra who has taken a pilgrimage to mecca (*haj*) | N |

*Semantic Domain: Customs and Rituals*

This domain lists the words for the customs and rituals that form the social and cultural foundations of the community. No direct counterparts of these words exists in Bangla.

**Table 3.8** ***Customs and rituals***

| No. | Ulti lexical item | Bangla counterpart | Meaning | Grammatical category |
|---|---|---|---|---|
| 67 | poncit̪ | – | panchayat | N |
| 68 | rot̪i | – | feast after *chalisa* (40th day after death) of a hijra, in their name | N |
| 69 | cɑt̪ɑi | – | a jury meeting to solve problems (while sitting on *catai*s or mats) | N |
| 70 | ɖɔn | – | penalty/ fine (in lakhs) | N |
| 71 | kɑlɑm | – | conversation/ discussion meeting on hijras' crimes/sins; panchayat | N |
| 72 | d̪ɑijɑr | – | house of a guru where small gatherings and meetings are held. | N |
| 73 | cit̪pɔn | – | jewellery pawned to the guru instead of paying penalty; security paid to go to *badhai* as an ad-hoc | N |
| 74 | ri:t̪ | – | the payment of a nominal amount and gifts as security money by the guru who wants to take a *caela* to their guru | N |
| 75 | rɑed̪ɑri | – | gift (cash or kind) given to respectable visitor of the house, especially, *naik* to *naik*. if not done properly, a don can be imposed | N |
| 76 | ɑnclɑ d̪ɛoɑ | – | an initiation ceremony where the guru drapes her *ancal* (end of her saree or a dupatta) over the new *caela's* head | V |
| 77 | ɖʰol cɔrɑno | – | to worship the *dhol* used for *badhai* | V |
| 78 | t̪ʰuke d̪ɛoɑ | – | to reject/ let go of a *caela* by their guru | V |

*Semantic Domain: Occupations*

The socially marginalized hijra community has survived for as long as it has by working in various non-conventional occupations to earn money. Of them, *bad̪$^{h}$ai* is exclusively done by the hijra community, while occupations like *c$^{h}$ɔlla*, *lɔgon* and *k$^{h}$ɑɟra* are common to cisgender people as well.

The suffix *-(b)ali* can combine with the nouns *bad̪$^{h}$ai*, *c$^{h}$ɔlla* and *k$^{h}$ɑɟra* to give us the adjectival forms *bad̪$^{h}$ai-ali*, *c$^{h}$ɔlla-bali*, and *k$^{h}$ɑɟra-bali*, which mean 'the who does (the job [noun])', respectively. The process can be represented thus:

| N + | (b)ɑli | → | Adj |
|---|---|---|---|
| (profession) | | | (professional) |

The domain of *c$^{h}$ɔlla* also contains words for 'train' (*corki*), 'ticket' (*patiya* – also the word for 'note'), 'ticket collector' (*patiya mashi*) and

**Table 3.9** ***Occupations***

| No. | Ulti lexical item | Bangla counterpart | Meaning | Grammatical category |
|---|---|---|---|---|
| 79 | bɑd̪$^{h}$ɑi | bɑccɑ nɑcɑno | to dance with and bless newborns for a living | N |
| 80 | fɑlijɑ | bɑccɑd̪er poʃɑk | baby clothes hung up to dry | N |
| 81 | ɟoubɔn | pɔn | money and gifts gotten in *badhai* | N |
| 82 | c$^{h}$ɔllɑ/mɑŋt̪i | b$^{h}$ikk$^{h}$e kɔrɑ | to beg for money | N |
| 83 | k$^{h}$ɑɟrɑ | ɟouno peʃɑ | sex-work | N |
| 84 | bɑrk$^{h}$ɑ | beʃʃɑ/ɟouno kormi | prostitute (woman or transgender who works for cash or kind) (refers to both individuals and groups) | N |
| 85 | b$^{h}$ɔk | beʃʃɑ | sex worker (refers to individuals) | N |
| 86 | bɑrk$^{h}$ɑ k$^{h}$ol | boiʃʃɑloe | brothel | N |
| 87 | bɑrk$^{h}$ɑ k$^{h}$ɑnɑ | boiʃʃɑloe | red-light area | N |
| 88 | ɟɔɟmɑn | grɑhok; ɟɔnot̪ɑ | client; public | N |
| 89 | lɔgon | bije | weddings where hijras and kotis are invited to perform in, mostly in Uttar Pradesh, Madhya Pradesh and Bihar. | N |
| 90 | c$^{h}$ɔmkɑno | nɑc kɔrɑ/nɑcɑ | to dance | N |

'clients/public' (*ɟɔɟman*), which, while not taboo, are essential to have code words for in this occupation. Similarly, other mainstream professions that Ulti has lexical items for are the 'police' (*dingor*), with whom the communities share a relationship of cautious antagonism, and 'sex worker' (*barkʰa, bʰɔk*, etc.), with whom they share a lot of common spaces and contexts, making the use of these terms relevant to the community's day-to-day experiences.

*Semantic Domain: Finance*

The domain of finance is an important one in Ulti. The lexical items include terminology not only for denominations of money, but also for the ways in which the earnings are divided in a hijra household. The earnings from *badhai* are divided into *ad̪ʰija*, which goes to the *daradin*, and *hissa,* which is the share of money each participating *caela* gets from the remaining half.

The word *ʈʰikri* is also used to refer to the hard clap that is associated with hijras by people outside the community. Hijras usually use the clap to emphasize a point, to intimidate a customer, or occasionally to non-verbally signal to each other in public places. It carries no specific meaning, contrary to popular belief; its use is interpreted exclusively based on the context.

**Table 3.10** ***Finance***

| No. | Ulti lexical item | Bangla counterpart | Meaning | Grammatical category |
|---|---|---|---|---|
| 91 | ɟʰɔlka | ʈaka | money | N |
| 92 | cillər | poeʃa | loose change | N |
| 93 | eʈi | d̪ɔʃ ʈaka | Rs 10 | N |
| 94 | haf gɔɟ | pɔncaʃ ʈaka | Rs 50 | N |
| 95 | gɔɟ; paʈʈi | ækʃo ʈaka | Rs 100 | N |
| 96 | ʈʰikʈi; ʈ̪ʰappu | haɟar ʈaka | Rs 1,000 | N |
| 97 | ʈeŋʈi | kuʈi haɟar ʈaka | Rs 20,000 | N |
| 98 | oli | puʈli | small purse for change (carried by a junior *caela* during *cholla*) | N |
| 99 | ad̪ʰija | – | one half of the total amount of the day's *badhai* earnings | N |
| 100 | hissa | – | the share of money each participating *caela* gets from the remaining half | N |

The word *eʈi* is also used to refer to the specific (vertical) way in which notes are folded while collecting money during *cholla*, which is noteworthy because in such scenarios, the currency note that is exchanged most commonly is the one for Rs 10. The reason Ulti does not have words for denominations larger than that is because, in the words of a koti, 'a hijra hardly ever sees that much money all at once'.

*Semantic Domain: Food and Intoxicants*

Food and intoxicants is an important domain in Ulti. The items comprise of rice, non-vegetarian food, alcohol, cigarettes and marijuana – which are either staple foods in the region, or whose names might need to be camouflaged in certain contexts for fear of public repercussion, like beef and intoxicants.

Besides these semantic domains, other domains in Ulti include abstract concepts such as 'being alive' (*jinda mashi*), 'health' (*tabiyat mashi*), colours (*laal mashi* 'red', *shaada mashi* 'white'), smells (*bhorkansi* 'stench', *boddo mashi* 'stench', *cishsha bhorkansi* 'aroma'), emotions (*khilpani* 'laughter', *rota mashi* 'crying', *bila batta* 'argument/insult', *korki* 'crazy'), 'house' (*khol*), 'mirror' (*shisha mashi, dorpon, aena*), 'water' (*jol mashi, wotar mashi, pani mashi*) and many more, all of which pertain to objects or ideas that are relevant to the immediate life of a hijra or koti.

Since the community has only begun to pursue education in recent years, there are practically no words for education except the complex verb *bidda mashi dharon kora* (to study/educate oneself), which is indicative of the

**Table 3.11** ***Food and intoxicants***

| No. | Ulti lexical item | Bangla counterpart | Meaning | Grammatical category |
|---|---|---|---|---|
| 101 | ʈakni | kʰabar | food | N |
| 102 | kʰelua | mɔd̪ | alcohol | N |
| 103 | d̪ʰumki | biɖi | cigarette | N |
| 104 | bila d̪ʰumki | ganɟa | marijuana | N |
| 105 | kʰolʃa | ɖim | egg | N |
| 106 | aʃ | macʰ | raw fish | N |
| 107 | bʰiʃant̪i | macʰ | cooked fish | N |
| 108 | kʰobra | maŋʃo | meat | N |
| 109 | aʈijal/ bɔrka kʰobra | gorur maŋʃo | beef | N |
| 110 | ciʃʃa kʰobra/ mʰæ | paʈʰa/kʰaʃir maŋʃo | mutton | N |

fact that the language is not developing as fast as the community is, and therefore does not reflect the real-life conditions or ideas of the community in most contexts. The community is multilingual, and their experiences go far beyond the limitations of domain and use indicated by the Ulti lexicon. In most cases, they simply switch to a language they are comfortable in (often Bangla, sometimes Hindi and English) to engage with discourses beyond the purview of the Ulti lexicon, which include politics, familial and financial issues, relationships, educational subjects, non-hijra professions, sports, entertainment and so on. Sometimes a noun from Bangla, Hindi/Urdu or English is borrowed and combined with the noun *mashi* to form a compound noun in Ulti. Examples include compounds with words borrowed from:

(a) **English**: *wɔʈar maʃi* (water), *hɛlo maʃi* (phone), *roɖ maʃi* (road)
(b) **Hindi**: *ɟind̪a maʃi* (alive), *d̪unija maʃi* (world), *d̪imag maʃi* (brain)
(c) **Bangla**: *bæbʃa maʃi* (business), *moɟa maʃi* (condom), *ʈana maʃi* (eyebrows)

Most of these compounds are endocentric compounds, but in some cases, they are exocentric. Examples include *ʈana maʃi* (eyebrows) where *ʈana* literally means ‘pulled’, *moɟa maʃi* (condom) where *moɟa* literally means ‘socks’, and *pat̪ʰor maʃi* (teeth) where *pat̪ʰor* literally means ‘stone’. In each of these cases, the original noun describes a property of the compound noun, such as its shape, function or its tensile strength. This is a very productive process used by the speakers to add new lexical items in Ulti. This process will be further elaborated upon in chapter 5.[4]

## *The Properties of Ulti*

All lexical items have certain phonological, semantic and syntactic properties. Following Koeneman and Zeijlstra (2017), these properties of a lexical item can be represented in a fundamental way as follows, as demonstrated by the example of the English lexical item, ‘hand’.

| | | | |
|---|---|---|---|
| 1 | *hand* | phonological properties | /hænɖ/ |
| | | semantic properties | hand |
| | | syntactic properties | being a noun (= [N]) |

In the above example, the first line carries the IPA transcription of the lexical item, which is its phonological property; the second line carries its meaning(s) representing its semantic property; and the third line carries its grammatical category (here, noun), which is its syntactic property. Following the same schemata, the lexical items of bare Ulti can be represented thus:

2 (a) Nouns

| | | | |
|---|---|---|---|
| (i) | *khumur* | phonological properties | /kʰumur/ |
| | | semantic properties | face<br>mouth |
| | | syntactic properties | being a noun (=[N]) |
| (ii) | *khol mashi* | phonological properties | /kʰol mɑʃi/ |
| | | semantic properties | house<br>room |
| | | syntactic properties | being a noun (=[N]) |
| (iii) | *jholka* | phonological properties | /ɟʰɔlkɑ/ |
| | | semantic properties | money |
| | | syntactic properties | being a noun (=[N]) |

(b) Verbs

| | | | |
|---|---|---|---|
| (i) | *pota* | phonological properties | /pɔt̪ɑ/ |
| | | semantic properties | to leave |
| | | syntactic properties | being a verb (=[V]) |
| (ii) | *sukhe neoa* | phonological properties | /ʃukʰe nɛoɑ/ |
| | | semantic properties | to claim somebody's<br>possession against<br>their wishes |
| | | syntactic properties | being a verb (=[V]) |
| (iii) | *tandi jhirano* | phonological properties | /ʈɑnɖi ɟʰirɑno/ |
| | | semantic properties | to beat someone up<br>to thrash |
| | | syntactic properties | being a verb (=[V]) |

(c) Pronouns

| | | | |
|---|---|---|---|
| (i) | *hamsi* | phonological properties | /həmsi/ |
| | | semantic properties | first person singular |
| | | syntactic properties | being a pronoun (=[PRO]) |
| (ii) | *tumsi* | phonological properties | /t̪umsi/ |
| | | semantic properties | second person singular |
| | | syntactic properties | being a pronoun (=[PRO]) |
| (iii) | *insi* | phonological properties | /ɪnsi/ |
| | | semantic properties | third person singular (proximal) |
| | | syntactic properties | being a pronoun (=[PRO]) |
| (iv) | *unsi* | phonological properties | /ʊnsi/ |
| | | semantic properties | third person singular (distal) |
| | | syntactic properties | being a pronoun (=[PRO]) |

(d) Demonstratives

| | | | |
|---|---|---|---|
| (i) | *insi* | phonological properties | /ɪnsi/ |
| | | semantic properties | this |

| | | | |
|---|---|---|---|
| | | syntactic properties | being a demonstrative (=[DEM]) |
| (ii) | *unsi* | phonological properties | /ʊnsi/ |
| | | semantic properties | that |
| | | syntactic properties | being a demonstrative (=[DEM]) |

(e) Adjectives

| | | | |
|---|---|---|---|
| (i) | *cissa* | phonological properties | /ciʃʃɑ/ |
| | | semantic properties | good<br>beautiful<br>happy<br>anything positive |
| | | syntactic properties | being an adjective (=[ADJ]) |
| (ii) | *bila* | phonological properties | /bilɑ/ |
| | | semantic properties | bad<br>ugly<br>upset<br>anything negative |
| | | syntactic properties | being an adjective (=[ADJ]) |
| (iii) | *ariyal* | phonological properties | /ɑɽijɑl/ |
| | | semantic properties | big in size or quantity |
| | | syntactic properties | being an adjective (=[ADJ]) |

(f) Adverbs

| | | | |
|---|---|---|---|
| (i) | *ariyal* | phonological properties | /ɑɽijɑl/ |
| | | semantic properties | very |
| | | syntactic properties | being an adverb (=[ADV]) |
| (ii) | *nathi* | phonological properties | /nɑt̪ʰi/ |
| | | semantic properties | no<br>negation |
| | | syntactic properties | being an adverb (=[ADV]) |
| (iii) | *utal* | phonological properties | /ut̪ɑl/ |
| | | semantic properties | very<br>only modifies ‘cissa’ |
| | | syntactic properties | being an adverb (=[ADV]) |

(g) Question_word

| | | | |
|---|---|---|---|
| (i) | *kinsi* | phonological properties | /kɪnsi/ |
| | | semantic properties | which |
| | | syntactic properties | being a question word (=[WH]) |

(h) Relative_pronoun

| | | | |
|---|---|---|---|
| (i) | *jinsi* | phonological properties | /ɟɪnsi/ |
| | | semantic properties | who |
| | | syntactic properties | being a relative pronoun (=[RP]) |

Most bare Ulti lexical items come from (an) unknown source(s). However, some of them can be traced to their regional counterparts like Farasi, Farsi, the Hyderabad variety or Dhaka Ulti, with whom they share certain common word roots. Some examples are provided in Table 3.12.

In this table, the Ulti lexical items have been transcribed in IPA but those from the other varieties have been reproduced in the same forms as they were originally documented by the respective researchers (Lahiry 2008; Nagar 2008; Awan and Sheeraz 2011b), with their respective meanings (in brackets). The meanings listed under the column named thus are the meanings of the Ulti words/lexical items. Wherever the meanings of the lexical items in the other varieties correspond to those of Ulti, their meanings have not been reproduced in brackets in the relevant boxes.

These are a handful of the many lexical items which share word roots across the hijra varieties spoken across the subcontinent, indicating that these languages exist in a linguistic continuum and have probably originated

**Table 3.12** ***Comparative analysis of Hijra lexical roots***

| | Ulti | U.P. Farasi | Pakistan Farsi | Dhaka Ulti | Meaning |
|---|---|---|---|---|---|
| 111 | ɑɽijɑl | adiyal (very) | arial (much/ very/long) | aariyal (big) | very/big/much |
| 112 | bilɑ | bila (bad/ wound) | beela (bad/thief/ dacoit/miser (M)) | billa (bad looking) | bad/ugly/sad/injury |
| 113 | ciʃʃɑ | cheesa (good) | chisa (beautiful/ good/lovely (M)) | chishya/chish | good/pretty/happy |
| 114 | cipʈi | sippo | seepo/sippo | chippu/sippu | vagina |
| 115 | likɔm/ likɑm | likkam | leekum/ leekar | likaam | penis |
| 116 | kʰumur | khomar* karna (to suck) | khomar (face) | – | mouth/face |
| 117 | kʰuʈni | khutni (back-biting/farasi) | khutni (back-biting) | khutni (back-biting) | talk |
| 118 | sʊɖɖʰi | suddi | suddi/sudhi | shuddi | old woman |
| 119 | ʈɑkni | taakni | taakni | takni (eating) | food |
| 120 | cɑmɑ | cham (liking) | cham (liking/ love/ understanding) | chaamo (excite the man to give him erection) | to take/see/hear/ understand |

*Note*: *in Ulti, *kʰumur kora* means 'to suck or give oral sex', just as it does in Farasi. But the speakers have reported that no word for 'mouth' exists in Farasi (Nagar 2008).

from a common source, diverging in form and meaning over time as a result of contact with the languages spoken in various regions. The common roots can usually be found in domains like the body, sexual organs and activities, and in grammatical categories like pronouns, adjectives and certain other nouns and verbs.

In Reddy's (2005) ethnographic study on hijras and kotis, we find one instance of a lexical item used in Hyderabad which shares a form across all the other varieties: *kadaa*. In Hyderabad, *kadaa chatla koti* refers to a koti who does not wear a saree (*catla*) and, in many cases, leads a closeted and dual life as, in Reddy's words, 'Kings by Day, Queens by Night' (ibid.: 63).

In Farasi, the same form appears in the phrase *kade taal ki koti*, and in Ulti, the corresponding phrase is *kora taal-er koti*. In both cases, the meaning of the phrase is the same as in the Hyderabad variety. In Pakistan's Hijra Farsi, *kade kera ho* is a command that translates to 'shut up/ be silent/ go away'. This phrase also appears in West Bengal Ulti and Dhaka Ulti as *kori kor* and *kari* (+V) respectively, both of which mean 'be quiet'. In West Bengal Ulti, *kori* also means 'secret', and the above-mentioned phrase is an imperative asking the addressee to be careful or discreet in the way they speak or act, to avoid detection or spilling a secret. This indicates that, even though as yet unresearched, there is evidence that the Hyderabad variety may also exist in the same linguistic continuum as the other varieties, which is further borne out by the fact that culturally, the hijra-koti tradition in Hyderabad has a lot of similarities with those in the other regions (Lahiry 2008; Nagar 2008; Awan and Sheeraz 2011b).

## Conclusion

A language like Ulti is as much a professional lect as a sociolect because the hijra community in particular is designed as a social system with specific professions, and the speakers are as much a social group as a professional group who live, work and spend most of their time together. This changes the way we consider professional lects in the literature, which are restricted to specific professional domains which are used at specific parts of the day. Ulti, on the other hand, is spoken in the non-professional domains of hijra life too – it is not restricted to the professional domain alone; it extends far beyond it. This makes it difficult to demarcate professional discourses in Ulti by time, place and interlocutors, like one can with other professional lects.

Further, the professional domain in Ulti consists of words that are used not just because of their technical specificity to the job, or to enable the speakers to index their positions as in-group members in the profession, but also to camouflage the group's conversations from the clients they are interacting with. This changes the way in which the data for such a lect are collected compared to other professional registers and lects, because the primary concern here must be to ensure the safety of the hijras and kotis and the secrecy of the language. Further, the community often denies permission to record their interactions at work, which is why such data, in my case, have been elicited second hand, through interviews and narrations. This lect necessitates an acute understanding of the hostile conditions in which these professions are performed, which becomes an important factor to consider while collecting as well as analysing the data for such a lect.

## Notes

1 Boa Sr. was the last living speaker of Bo, a Great Andamanese language. After her death, the language became extinct. The only knowledge of Bo that we have access to today is due to Abbi's (2013) documentation of the sounds, words and grammar of the language.

2 The revival of Hebrew as a spoken language in the late nineteenth century is a rare but famous example of how a dead language can be revitalized by, among other means, creating a dictionary of the language and using it as a medium of instruction in classrooms. See 'How to Revive an Ancient Language, According to 19th-century Hebrew and Persian Revivalists', UW Stroum Center for Jewish Studies, https://jewishstudies.washington.edu/israel-hebrew/reviving-hebrew-persian-ancient-languages-eliezer-ben-yehuda-manekji-limji-hataria/, accessed 25 May 2023.

3 See https://en.wikipedia.org/wiki/Lexicography, accessed 26 December 2020.

4 Also see Fabb (2001), Aronoff and Fudeman (2011).

# 4

# Embedding Ulti

## A Grammatical Analysis

In the previous chapter, we looked at the lexical items of Ulti and the semantic domains they are used in. Here, we will examine the ways in which these lexical items combine and embed themselves in the Bangla syntactic framework to form Ulti sentences, following Myers-Scotton's Matrix Language Framework (MLF) for bilingual code-switching.

The first section is a theoretical overview of the code-switching literature in sociolinguistics. The MLF model for bilingual code-switching presented in the second section is used to analyse how content morphemes from bare Ulti embed themselves in the grammatical frame of the matrix language Bangla in the nominal, verbal and negation phrases. We also observe the emergence and function of the system morpheme *-unsi* in the verbal paradigm and the development of the negation marker *nathi* alongside the Bangla negation marker *na*, which provide valuable evidence that Ulti is linguistically expanding and developing system morphemes of its own; and if the language continues expanding thus, it might eventually lead to a decrease in its reliance on Bangla system morphemes and a grammatical structure distinct and independent from the grammar it currently shares with Bangla. The third section is an extract from an Ulti conversation in a natural setting that demonstrates examples of most of the features and code-switching phenomena discussed in the chapter.

### Code-switching in Sociolinguistics: An Overview

Code-switching as a phenomenon has generated much scholarly attention, from discursive analyses of conversational code-switching data to discussions on speakers' motivations for code-switching, to formal analyses of code-switched utterances. One of the first scholars to work on language alternation in linguistic anthropology was Barker (1947), who sought to understand the contexts and motivations for switching between languages in the Mexican-American community in Tucson, Arizona. He was the first to identify language choice in such interactions as a matter of situational requirements as well as a marker of one's identity, and to analyse bilingualism itself to be a marker of one's cosmopolitan identity.

The first person credited with using the term 'code-switching' in linguistics is Vogt (1954), in his article 'Language Contacts', which was heavily inspired by Weinreich's (1953) book *Languages in Contact* (Alvarez-Cáccamo 1998; Benson 2001; Nilep 2006). Vogt characterizes code-switching as a psychological rather than a linguistic phenomenon that is common to languages in contact and whose motivations are extralinguistic. Yet, he argues, it is of 'great interest to the linguist because it is the condition of . . . the interference between languages' (Vogt 1954: 368, quoted in Nilep 2006: 5).

One of the most seminal works on code-switching is Blom and Gumperz's (1972) article 'Social Meaning in Linguistic Structures', which explored code-switching between two distinct codes of Norwegian – Bokmål and Ranamål – which are distinguished by minor phonological, morphological and lexical differences, and perform separate social functions. It is noteworthy that the kind of code-switching characterized here, as well as in Gumperz's earlier work on varieties of Hindi in northern India (Gumperz 1958, 1961, 1964a, 1964b), focus on code-switching between varieties of one language rather than two distinct languages, especially when one variety is considered the standard and occupies an elevated social role and significance.

This is most relevant to this research, where Ulti and Bangla can also be characterized as varieties of the same language with merely some lexical and morphological differences that perform distinct social functions, with Bangla occupying a sociopolitical position as the official language of the state of West Bengal that is much higher than that of Ulti, a secret language spoken by a minority group. In his earlier work on Hindi varieties, Gumperz – following Ervin-Tripp (1964) in her analysis of bilingual behaviour in Japanese-American women – had described that the choice of language by bilingual speakers was influenced by factors such as interlocutors, setting and topic of conversation. Blom and Gumperz argued that these factors '"restrict the selection of linguistic variables" in a manner that is somewhat analogous to syntactic or semantic restrictions. That is, in particular social situations, some linguistic forms may be more appropriate than others' (Nilep 2006: 7).

These three factors play a major role in determining the choice to use Ulti in social situations. Ulti is spoken amongst fellow Ulti speakers, most often in a setting that comprises only community insiders, or is spoken by community members in public in a manner designed to camouflage the contents of their speech from the mainstream public. The topic of conversation in hijra and koti interactions imposes a further constraint on the choice of language for the Ulti speaker, because, as discussed in the previous chapter, the Ulti lexicon specifically comprises words in certain domains that lack the corresponding Bangla words. Hence, even in intra-community interactions, only Bangla can be used to discuss topics in the domain of music, education, health and so on, while only Ulti can be used in certain other conversations, most notably pertaining to the domain of professions, customs and relationships intrinsic to the hijra social system. There are certain other domains like travel, food, adornments, (most) body parts, etc., that have lexical items in both Bangla and Ulti, which allows the speakers to alternate freely between the languages when discussing these subjects.

Blom and Gumperz (1972) argue, however, that these choices of code by the speaker are intentional in the social meaning and message they choose to convey; they are not just a function of content or context, but also of what Gumperz (1982) terms 'discourse strategies'. Myers-Scotton (1993a) expands the idea of discourse strategies to include 'dynamic' factors such as the length and nature of the relationship between the interlocutors, and to assess 'whether power or solidarity is salient' in these equations. In the case of Ulti, the choice to use it is not just a marker and an exercise of power within the community, but is also intended to convey and engender solidarity amongst the community members. Ulti conveys power and solidarity in a subculture that has emerged in response to the dominant conservative culture where Bangla (and English) holds a position of immense power and influence, which has been harnessed to ideologically and socioeconomically exclude the community from mainstream society. This dynamic has been described by Heller thus: 'Dominant groups rely on norms of language choice to maintain symbolic domination, while subordinate groups may use code switching to resist or redefine the value of symbolic resources in the linguistic marketplace' (Heller 1992, 1995, as paraphrased by Nilep 2006: 13).

Heller, in her study of anglophones in Quebec and Ontario, highlighted the economics of bilingualism and analysed code-switching as a political strategy (Heller 1988b, 1992, 1995, 1999). 'Since languages tend to become associated with idealized situations and groups of speakers, the use of multiple languages "permits people to say and do, indeed to *be* two or more things where normally a choice is expected"' (Heller 1988b: 93, quoted in Nilep 2006: 12). This theory not only places the speaker at the centre of the interaction, but foregrounds their subjectivity and multiplicity of identities that most other such studies tend to overlook. This assertion is corroborated by the multilingual behaviour of the speakers of Ulti, whose linguistic choices and behaviour are indexical of their composite – and often contesting – identities.

While Heller's work focuses on the reasons behind and effects of code-switching across class lines, the works of Nishimura (1992), Rampton (1995), Bucholtz (1999), Lo (1999), Jaffe (2000), Bailey (2001, 2002), and Torras and Gafaranga (2002) examine code-switching across racial, ethnic and linguistic groups. Bailey demonstrates that the Dominican American second-generation youth residing in Rhode Island construct their cultural and ethnic identity as non-White and non-Black by 'shifting uses of nonstandard Dominican Spanish, Caribbean Spanish, African American Vernacular English, and other nonstandard English varieties' (Nilep 2006: 14, summarizing Bailey 2001, 2002). This research takes the exploration of language and identity further by examining the code-switching behaviour of a social group who are not just gender and sexual minorities, but also sociopolitical and economic minorities on the basis of their class and caste identities and geographical location.

Most scholars agree that the phenomenon of code-switching can be broadly defined as 'the use of more than one language in the course of a single communicative episode' (Heller 1988a: 1). While these definitions have been drawn from Gumperz (1982), they depart from his with the introduction of the term 'language' to replace the phrase 'different grammatical systems or subsystems'. Gumperz (ibid.: 59) states that 'conversational code switching can be defined as the juxtaposition within the same speech exchange of passages of speech belonging to two different grammatical systems or subsystems'. As the difference between a language and a grammatical (sub) system has not been clearly defined here, it is best to treat them as separate categories for now.

This definition entails that the phenomenon of code-switching between Bangla and Ulti need not be analysed as a unique phenomenon involving one language and one set of lexical items (as proposed in chapter 1); following Gumperz, we can also consider it to be an instance of code-switching between a language (Bangla) and a grammatical (sub)system of Bangla (Ulti), where Ulti is characterized as a variety or register of Bangla, which is not a unique phenomenon. However, in order to establish that Ulti is indeed a variety or register of Bangla with a grammar that is similar yet divergent from

Bangla's, we need to first analyse the features of the grammatical system of Ulti. The best way to accomplish this would be to follow our initial proposal and look at Ulti as a mixed language where lexical items from bare Ulti are embedded in the grammatical framework of the matrix language Bangla, following Myers-Scotton's (1993b, 1997) MLF model. What the inferences from this analysis tell us about Ulti and whether it can be characterized as a language, a grammatical (sub)system, or a variety or register of Bangla, is a question that will be explored in detail in chapter 6.

## The Matrix Language Framework

Myers-Scotton has worked extensively on the phenomenon of code-switching, focusing on both its sociolinguistic and structural aspects, and formulating theories that could best explain how and why bilingual code-switching occurs. Bilingual speech has been defined as the presence of 'surface level morphemes from two or more language varieties in the same clause. With the 4-M model, the Uniform Structure Principle (USP) clarifies and strengthens the Matrix Language Framework (MLF) model, as a model of codeswitching' (Myers-Scotton and Jake 2009: 336).

According to the USP, bilingual code-switching or code-mixing demonstrates an asymmetry between 'the participating languages and morpheme types at a number of abstract levels': the matrix language (ML) contributes the structural framework and system morphemes and plays a dominating role in the bilingual clause, while the embedded language (EL) contributes the content morphemes and phrases that embed themselves in the framework of the ML and are governed by the grammatical rules of the ML 'if they meet EL well-formedness conditions, as well as those ML (well-formedness) conditions applying to the clause as a whole (e.g. phrase placement)' (Jake, Myers-Scotton and Gross 2002, quoted in Myers-Scotton and Jake 2009: 337).

In the code-mixed language Ulti, the grammatical frame and system morphemes are provided by the ML Bangla while the content morphemes are provided by bare Ulti, which acts as the EL in this context. In the example set below, the examples marked (i) present the Ulti sentences with Ulti content morphemes highlighted in bold, while those marked (ii) present the corresponding Bangla sentences with the Bangla content morphemes corresponding to the Ulti ones in (i) placed within square brackets.

| | | | | | | |
|---|---|---|---|---|---|---|
| 1 (a) | (i) | **həmsi-r** | **ɟ$^h$orni** | harie | g-ɛ-c$^h$-e | (Ulti) |
| | (ii) | [ama]-r | [gɔjna] | harie | g-ɛ-c$^h$-e | (Bangla) |
| | | 1PS.Gen | jewellery | lose | go.Pft.Pst.3P | |
| | | 'I've lost my jewellery.' | | | | |
| (b) | (i) | ona-r | **k$^h$ulpi**-ṯa | ki | **bila** | (Ulti) |
| | (ii) | ona-r | [ɟuṯo]-ṯa | ki | [baɟe] | (Bangla) |
| | | 3PS.Gen | shoes.Cla | so | bad | |
| | | 'Their (sg.) shoes are so ugly.' | | | | |
| (c) | (i) | **piṯ maʃi**-ke | **k$^h$ol**-e | **pɔṯ**-i-e | a-e | (Ulti) |
| | (ii) | [b$^h$ai/bon]-ke | [baṟi]-ṯe | [rek$^h$]-e | a-e | (Bangla) |
| | | sibling.Dat | house.Loc | leave.(Caus).Cpm | come.2P | |
| | | 'Drop (your) sibling home and come.' | | | | |
| (d) | (i) | **corki**-ṯa | **-ʊnsi** | **pɔn**-e | ɟa-c-c$^h$-e | (Ulti) |
| | (ii) | [ṯren]-ṯa | [oi] | [ḏik]-e | ɟa-c-c$^h$-e | (Bangla) |
| | | train.Cla | that | side.Loc | go.Prog.Pres.3P | |
| | | 'The train is going that way.' | | | | |

In these examples we see that the content morphemes from bare Ulti could be a noun (such as *ɟ$^h$orni, k$^h$ulpi, piṯ maʃi, k$^h$ol, corki* in examples 1a-i to d-i); a verb (such as *pɔṯ-* in example 1c-i); an adjective (such as *bila* in example 1b-i); a pronoun (such as *həmsi* in example 1a-i); or a demonstrative (such as *-ʊnsi pɔn* in example 1d-i). But the system morphemes in the sentence, including inflectional markers, agreement markers, case markers and classifiers, all come from the ML Bangla. Comparing example sets (i) and (ii), we see that the Ulti content morphemes embed themselves in the Bangla grammatical framework and combine with the system morphemes in the same way as the Bangla content morphemes do. In other words, the Ulti content words or lexical items are syntactically and semantically similar to their Bangla counterparts.

Given that bare Ulti has no grammatical framework that can be considered separate from Bangla, and that the grammatical frame of Ulti can only come from Bangla, we can classify Ulti as an example of Classic code-switching (Classic CS), but with a caveat: it is an instance of code-switching between a language and a set of lexical items, not between two participating languages.

Classic CS has been defined as 'codeswitching in which empirical evidence shows that abstract grammatical structure within a clause comes from only one of the participating languages'. This is presented in contrast to Composite CS, which is 'the abstract grammatical structure underlying surface configurations still comes largely from one language, but also partially from another' (Myers-Scotton and Jake 2009: 339; see also Myers-Scotton and Jake 2001 and Jake, Myers-Scotton and Gross 2002).

**Table 4.1** ***The 4-M morphemes***

| Types of morphemes | Examples |
|---|---|
| Early SMs | plural affixes, verb satellites, derivational affixes, determiners |
| Late SM: Bridges | the associative or possessive element that occurs between a possessor noun and the element that is possessed: English – of, 's |
| Late SM: Outsiders | agreement markers, case markers |

The two fundamental principles on which the MLF is based are the Morpheme Order Principle (MOP) and the System Morpheme Principle (SMP). The MOP posits that 'in mixed constituents consisting of at least one Embedded Language word and any number of Matrix Language morphemes, surface word (and morpheme) order will be that of the Matrix Language'. The SMP states that 'in Matrix Language + Embedded Language constituents, all system morphemes which have grammatical relations external to their head constituents (i.e., which participate in the sentence's thematic role grid) will come from the Matrix Language' (Myers-Scotton 2006: 244). Both these principles are adequately fulfilled in Ulti (as demonstrated in example set 1), not least because the EL in this case has no system morphemes, and therefore no grammatical structure of its own.

The 4-M model augments the MLF model by classifying the morphemes that come into play in code-switching into three types of system morphemes: early system morphemes (SMs) and two types of late SMs, namely bridges and outsiders. 'The MLF model's SMP is often misunderstood as applying to all SMs. However, it was always intended to constrain only one type of SM, now called outsiders' (Myers-Scotton 1993a, 1997: 82, cited in Myers-Scotton and Jake 2009: 341). This model is primarily concerned with 'viewing the morphemes in terms of their syntactic roles and how they are activated in language production' (Myers-Scotton and Jake 2009: 341). It primarily distinguishes between 'morphemes that are conceptually activated (e.g., nouns and verbs) and those that are structurally-assigned (e.g., AGR elements)'. Besides content morphemes:

> [e]arly SMs (e.g., plural affixes) are also conceptually-activated; they flesh out the meaning of their content morpheme heads that 'indirectly elect' them (see Bock and Levelt 1994). Because they are structurally-assigned, late SMs contrast with both content morphemes and early SMs in an important way.

> . . . While early SMs largely build semantic structure, late SMs build syntactic structure. (Ibid.: 341–44)

The types of morphemes according to the 4-M model have been classified as in Table 4.1.

The following sections explore in greater detail the nature of these morphemes and the manner in which they come into operation in Ulti.

## *The Nominal Paradigm*

### *Nouns and Noun Phrases*

Any sentence with even one bare Ulti content morpheme can be considered an Ulti sentence. Nouns in Ulti occur as bare nouns which optionally make compounds with *mashi*, obligatory *mashi* compound nouns (as will be elaborated in chapter 5), or as noun phrases. In the following example set, the relevant Ulti nouns and noun phrases (examples (i), highlighted in bold and demarcated within square brackets) appear as the subject (2a), direct object (2b), indirect object (2c) or adjunct (2d) in a sentence. Their corresponding Bangla sentences have been presented in (ii). Since the nouns in the Ulti examples optionally compound with *mashi*, they have been placed within parentheses. This indicates that whether or not the noun appears in its bare form or as a *mashi* compound, it participates in the same way in the sentence.

| 2(a) (i) | [**ʊnsi** | ragi | **suḍḍʰa (maʃi)**] | ama-ke | ḍak-cʰ-e | (Ulti) |
|---|---|---|---|---|---|---|
| (ii) | [oi | ragi | bʰɔdrolok] | ama-ke | ḍak-cʰ-e | (Bangla) |
| | that | angry | old man.3PS | 1PS.Dat | call.Pres.3P | |

‘That angry old man is calling me.’

| (b) (i) | am-ra | [o-r | **corki (maʃi)**-ṭa-ke] | bila | kor-e-cʰ-i | (Ulti) |
|---|---|---|---|---|---|---|
| (ii) | am-ra | [o-r | gaḍi-ṭa-ke] | nɔʃṭo | kor-e-cʰ-i | (Bangla) |
| | 1P.PlCla | 3PS.Gen | car.Cla.Dat | damage | do.Pft.Pres.1P | |

‘We have damaged their(Sg.) car.’

| (c) (i) | bɔni | ama-ke | [æk-ṭa | **ʃat̪ra (maʃi)**] | di-e-cʰ-e | (Ulti) |
|---|---|---|---|---|---|---|
| (ii) | bɔni | ama-ke | [æk-ṭa | ʃaṛi] | di-e-cʰ-e | (Bangla) |
| | Boni.3PS | 1PS.Dat | one | saree | give.Pft.Pres.3P | |

‘Boni has given me a saree.’

| (d) (i) | raɟu | [**corki (maʃi)**-t̪e] | bou-ke | ḍalmuṭ | kʰa-i-e-cʰ-e | (Ulti) |
|---|---|---|---|---|---|---|
| (ii) | raɟu | [ṭren-e] | bou-ke | ḍalmuṭ | kʰa-i-e-cʰ-e | (Bangla) |
| | Raju.3PS | train.Loc | wife.Dat | snacks | eat.Caus.Pft.Pres.3P | |

‘Raju fed his wife snacks in the train.’

In example 2(a-i), we find that the Ulti noun phrase ‘*ʊnsi ragi suḍḍʰa (maʃi)*' does not comprise completely of Ulti content morphemes. The adjective *ragi* (angry) is a Bangla content morpheme that is used in the NP because Ulti has no lexical item for angry. Since bare Ulti has no grammar of its own, the question of EL islands existing in the abstract grammatical framework of bare Ulti and meeting EL well-formedness conditions is redundant. Instead, we find that the Ulti noun phrase is also governed by the grammatical rules of the ML Bangla, as can be corroborated by comparing it with the structure of the NP '*oi ragi bʰɔdrolok*' in example 2(a-ii).

However, it must be noted that bare Ulti and Bangla content morphemes mostly occur in free variation in Ulti; any content morpheme in any clause or phrase in an Ulti sentence can come from either Bangla or bare Ulti (or sometimes be borrowed from Hindi or English), regardless of the other constituents in the sentence. Such variation does not have any syntactic consequence on the sentence. This is illustrated in example 2(b), where the NP '*or corki (maʃi)-ʈa-ke*' has a Bangla demonstrative and a bare Ulti noun. There is no selectional restriction with regard to source language in Ulti: whether the demonstrative and noun combination in this NP is Bangla-Ulti, Ulti-Bangla, Ulti-Ulti or Bangla-Bangla, the resultant sentence will remain the same, as shown in 2(e).

| | | | | | | |
|---|---|---|---|---|---|---|
| (e) (i) | ɑm-rɑ | [o-r | **corki (mɑʃi)**-ʈɑ-ke] | bilɑ | kor-e-cʰ-i | (Ulti) |
| (ii) | ɑm-rɑ | [**ʊnsi**-r | **corki (mɑʃi)**-ʈɑ-ke] | nɔʃʈo | kor-e-cʰ-i | (Ulti) |
| (iii) | ɑm-rɑ | [**ʊnsi**-r | gɑɖi-ʈɑ-ke] | bilɑ | kor-e-cʰ-i | (Ulti) |
| (iv) | ɑm-rɑ | [o-r | gɑɖi-ʈɑ-ke] | nɔʃʈo | kor-e-cʰ-i | (Bangla) |
| | 1P.PlCla | 3PS.Gen | car.Cla.Dat | damage | do.Pft.Pres.1P | |
| | 'We have damaged their(sg.) car.' | | | | | |

*Classifiers and Case Markers*

In the above examples we also see that the Bangla system morphemes like classifiers and case markers attach to the bare Ulti content morphemes (with or without *mashi*) in the same manner and in the same order as with Bangla content morphemes: in the form of suffixes with the case marker following the classifier. Further examples of Bangla classifiers and case markers attaching to Ulti content morphemes are given below.

*Classifiers*

In the following examples, the classifiers have been highlighted in bold in both the Ulti and Bangla examples. From the set of classifiers in Bangla, only *-ʈa* (3a), *-gulo* (3b and 3c) and *-ra* (3d), which are most widely used in Bangla, can attach to Ulti lexical items. The less common classifiers like

*-ɟɔn*, *-kʰana* and *-kʰani* attach only to Bangla lexical items, not Ulti. As noted above, in NPs where both appear, the classifier attaches to the noun first, followed by the case marker in both Ulti and Bangla.

| 3 (a) (i) | kot̪i-**ʈɑ** | kʰɑuri | ɟog | ɟur-e-cʰ-e | | (Ulti) |
|---|---|---|---|---|---|---|
| (ii) | kot̪i-**ʈɑ** | fɔls | cul | lɑgi-e-cʰ-e | | (Bangla) |
| | koti.Cla | fake | hair | wear.Pft.Pres.3P | | |
| | 'The koti has worn a wig.' | | | | | |

| (b) (i) | ʃɔb | kot̪i-**gulo**-ke | mɑŋt̪i | kort̪e | pɑʈʰ-ɑ | (Ulti) |
|---|---|---|---|---|---|---|
| (ii) | ʃɔb | kot̪i-**gulo**-ke | bʰikkʰɑ | kort̪e | pɑʈʰ-ɑ | (Bangla) |
| | all | koti.PlCla.Dat | beg | do | send.2P | |
| | 'Send all the kotis to beg for alms.' | | | | | |

| (c) (i) | t̪onnɑ-**gulo**-r | kʰumur-**gulo** | ɑʈijɑl | bilɑ | d̪ekʰt̪e | (Ulti) |
|---|---|---|---|---|---|---|
| (ii) | cʰele-**gulo**-r | mukʰ-**gulo** | kʰub | bɑɟe | dekʰt̪e | (Bangla) |
| | boy.PlCla.Gen | face.PlCla | very | bad | see | |
| | 'The faces of the boys are really ugly.' | | | | | |

| (d) (i) | həmsi-**rɑ** | kɑlke | ɟɔepur mɑʃi-t̪e | pot̪-b-o | (Ulti) |
|---|---|---|---|---|---|
| (ii) | ɑm-**rɑ** | kɑlke | ɟɔepur-e | ɟɑ-b-o | (Bangla) |
| | 1P.PlCla | tomorrow | Jaipur.Loc | leave.Fut.1P | |
| | 'We will go to Jaipur tomorrow.' | | | | |

In examples 3(b–d), the subject is an Ulti content morpheme with a Bangla system morpheme – the plural classifiers *-ra* and *-gulo*. Even though plural morphemes are supposed to be early SMs and can come from the EL, the absence of any kind of plural marker in bare Ulti necessitates that Ulti plurals must always form with the help of Bangla classifiers.

*Case Markers*

The following examples illustrate how the different case markers (highlighted in bold) attach to Ulti content morphemes and their Bangla counterparts. Case markers are outsider late SMs and always come from the ML – a pattern that is certainly not violated in Ulti. From the examples below, we see that all the Bangla case markers, i.e. accusative (4a), dative (4b), genitive (4b and d), locative (4c and d), comitative (4c), ablative (4e) and instrumental (4f), behave in exactly the same manner in Bangla (ii) and Ulti (i).

| 4 (a) (i) | t̪umsi | ʊnsi-**ke** | cʰɔmkɑt̪e | kʰoʈ-o | (Ulti) |
|---|---|---|---|---|---|
| (ii) | t̪umi | o-**ke** | nɑct̪e | bɔl-o | (Bangla) |
| | 2PS | 3PS.Acc | dance | tell.2P | |
| | 'Ask them(sg.) to dance.' | | | | |

| | | | | | | | |
|---|---|---|---|---|---|---|---|
| (b) (i) | ʈæpkɑ-ʈɑ | ʊnsi-**r** | piʈ lahɑran-**ke** | boi | d̪i-e-cʰ-e | | (Ulti) |
| (ii) | cʰele-ʈɑ | o-**r** | bon-**ke** | boi | d̪i-e-cʰ-e | | (Bangla) |
| | boy | 3PS.Gen | sister.Dat | book | give.Pft.Pres.3P | | |

'The boy gave a book to his sister.'

| | | | | | | | | | |
|---|---|---|---|---|---|---|---|---|---|
| (c) (i) | ɑmi | hælo mɑʃi-t̪e | æk-ʈɑ | ʈonnɑ-**r** | **ʃɑt̪ʰe** | kʰuʈni | kʰuʈ-i | | (Ulti) |
| (ii) | ɑmi | fon-**e** | æk-ʈɑ | cʰele-**r** | **ʃɑt̪ʰe** | kɔt̪ʰɑ | bol-i | | (Bangla) |
| | 1PS | phone.Loc | one.Cla | boy.Gen | Com | talk | talk.1P | | |

'I spoke with a boy over the phone.'

| | | | | | | |
|---|---|---|---|---|---|---|
| (d) (i) | ɔpiʃ-**e** | ʊnsi-**r** | kɔrmo | mɑʃi | ciʃʃɑ | (Ulti) |
| (ii) | ɔpiʃ-**e** | o-**r** | kɑɟ | | bʰɑlo | (Bangla) |
| | office.Loc | 3PS.Gen | work | | good | |

'Their(sg.) work in the office is good.'

| | | | | | | |
|---|---|---|---|---|---|---|
| (e) (i) | o-**d̪er** | **t̪ʰeke** | ɟʰɔlkɑ | ɟʰir-i | ɑʈijɑl | (Ulti) |
| (ii) | o-**d̪er** | **t̪ʰeke** | ʈakɑ | ne-i | kʰub | (Bangla) |
| | 3P.PlClaGen | Abl | money | take.1P | much | |

'I take a lot of money from them.'

| | | | | | | |
|---|---|---|---|---|---|---|
| (f) (i) | ʊnsi-**ke** | **d̪ije** | bɒblu-**ke** | goʃol | kɔr-ɑ-o | (Ulti) |
| (ii) | o-**ke** | **d̪ije** | bɒblu-**ke** | snɑn | kɔr-ɑ-o | (Bangla) |
| | 3PS.Acc | Ins | Bablu.Dat | bath | do.Caus.2P | |

'Make them(sg.) give Bablu a bath.'

In examples 4(b) and 4(d), we also see instances of the genitive marker *-r*, which is a bridge late SM. As expected, in Ulti this morpheme comes exclusively from Bangla.

*Pronouns and Demonstratives*

Ulti has lexical items for all the pronouns and demonstratives, which behave in very interesting ways. While they act like their Bangla counterparts in the way they form plurals (with classifiers), take case markers, etc., they diverge in one aspect: pronouns and demonstratives in Ulti can optionally form compounds with *mashi*. This compound then behaves in the same manner in a sentence as bare pronouns and demonstratives in Ulti. Below are examples of bare pronouns (in bold) in Ulti (i) and Bangla (ii): first person (5a), second person (5b), third person proximal (5c) and third person distal (5d).

*Pronouns*

| | | | | | |
|---|---|---|---|---|---|
| 5 (a) (i) | **həmsi** | rɑni-ke | ɟʰɔlkɑ | pɑʈʰi-e-cʰ-i | (Ulti) |
| (ii) | **ɑmi** | rɑni-ke | ʈakɑ | pɑʈʰi-e-cʰ-i | (Bangla) |
| | 1PS | Rani.Dat | money | send.Pft.Pres.1P | |

'I have sent money to Rani.'

| | | | | | |
|---|---|---|---|---|---|
| (b) (i) | **t̪umsi**-ra | həmsi-r | kʰol-e | pɔt̪-o | (Ulti) |
| (ii) | **t̪om**-ra | ama-r | gʰɔr-e | ɟa-o | (Bangla) |
| | 2P.PlCla | 1PS.Gen | house.Loc | leave.2P | |
| | 'You all go to my house.' | | | | |

| | | | | | |
|---|---|---|---|---|---|
| (c) (i) | **ɪnsi**-r | kʰol maʃi | bila | ho-e-cʰ-e | (Ulti) |
| (ii) | **e**-r | pet̪ | kʰarap | ho-e-cʰ-e | (Bangla) |
| | 3PS.Gen | tummy | bad | be.Pft.Pres.3P | |
| | 'Their(sg.) tummy is upset.' | | | | |

| | | | | | | |
|---|---|---|---|---|---|---|
| (d) (i) | **ʊnsi**-d̪er | mod̪d̪ʰe | aɽijal | t̪anda-t̪and̪i | hɔ-e | (Ulti) |
| (ii) | **o**-d̪er | mod̪d̪ʰe | kʰub | mara-mari | hɔ-e | (Bangla) |
| | 3P.PlGen | between | much | fighting | be.3P | |
| | 'They always get involved in physical fights with each other.' | | | | | |

*Demonstratives*

The following are examples of bare demonstratives (highlighted in bold) in Ulti (i) and Bangla (ii), where (5e) shows the proximal demonstrative and (5f) shows the distal one.

| | | | | | | |
|---|---|---|---|---|---|---|
| (e) (i) | **ɪnsi** | kʰulpi | na | ɟurle-i | ciʃʃa | (Ulti) |
| (ii) | **ei** | ɟut̪o | na | porle-i | bʰalo | (Bangla) |
| | This | shoe | Neg | wear.Emp | good | |
| | 'It is best if you don't wear these shoes.' | | | | | |

| | | | | | | |
|---|---|---|---|---|---|---|
| (f) (i) | **ʊnsi** | pɔn-e | aɽijal | bilt̪al | leg-e-cʰ-e | (Ulti) |
| (ii) | **oi** | d̪ik-e | biʃal | ɟʰɔgra | leg-e-cʰ-e | (Bangla) |
| | That | side.Loc | big | fight | start.Pft.Pres.3P | |
| | 'A big fight has erupted there.' | | | | | |

The noun *mashi* can select a nominal from any language to form a compound with. Examples include *mashi* compounds formed with Ulti, Bangla, English and Hindi nouns (discussed in detail in chapter 5). However, when it comes to pronouns and demonstratives, *mashi* can only form compounds with the Ulti lexical items; doing so with the Bangla ones gives an ungrammaticality reading (indicated with * in the examples below and henceforth):

| 6 | Ulti | Bangla | Gloss | Grammatical category |
|---|---|---|---|---|
| (a) | həmsi maʃi | *ami maʃi | 1PS | pronoun |
| (b) | t̪ʊmsi maʃi | *t̪umi maʃi | 2PS | pronoun |
| (c) | ɪnsi maʃi | *e maʃi | 3PS (Prox) | pronoun |
| (d) | ʊnsi maʃi | *o maʃi | 3PS (Dist) | pronoun |
| (e) | ɪnsi maʃi | *ei maʃi | this | demonstrative |
| (f) | ʊnsi maʃi | *oi maʃi | that | demonstrative |

These *mashi* compounds then behave in exactly the same manner in a sentence as their bare counterparts, just as nominal *mashi* compounds behave identically to their bare noun counterparts. However, this establishes that the pronouns and demonstratives in Ulti are distinct from their Bangla counterparts in their ability to form compounds with *mashi*. But since *mashi* carries neither any (in)definiteness feature nor interferes with the grammatical structure or semantic import of a sentence, this distinction does not have any far-reaching implications on the syntax or on the nature of code-switching in Ulti.

## *The Verbal Paradigm*

Ulti verbs can appear in many forms, from simplex to complex verbs, where either both the main verb and light verb are bare Ulti lexical items, or where the main verb is from Ulti and the light verb is from Bangla. Ulti sentences do not necessarily always have Ulti verb phrases, though; very often they have Bangla simplex and complex verbs. There is no instance of complex verbs where the main verb is from Bangla and the light verb from Ulti. Examples of Ulti verb types include:

| | | |
|---|---|---|
| 7 (i) Simplex verbs: | d̪ʰurɑno (to have sex) | |
| | pɔt̪ɑ (to leave) | |
| | kʰuʈɑ (to tell/speak) | |
| (ii) Complex verbs: | ʃukʰe nɛoɑ (to claim something) | (U+B) |
| | kʰumur kɔrɑ (to have oral sex) | (U+B) |
| | cipʈi d̪ʰurɑno (to have vaginal sex) | (U+U) |
| | ɟʰinni pɔt̪ɑno (to masturbate) | (U+U) |
| | cɑmɑcɑmi kɔrɑ (to seduce) | (U+B) |
| | bid̪d̪ɑ mɑʃi d̪ʰɑron kɔrɑ (to study) | (U+B+B) |

The verb phrase in Ulti, regardless of which language its verb roots come from, always inflect for tense, aspect and agree for person and honorificity through the Bangla system morphemes, as elaborated in the following sections.

### *Agreement*

Agreement markers in bilingual codeswitching are outsider late SMs which always come from the matrix language. Ulti verbs, just like Bangla verbs, agree only for person and honorificity, not for number or gender. However, unlike Bangla which has three levels of honorificity, Ulti shows only two levels of (non-)honorific agreement on the verb: the informal and the intimate. The highest and formal level of honorificity does not exist in Ulti as the speakers find it counter-intuitive to the nature of the relationships and interactions in the community, which is of an informal, familial nature irrespective of the hierarchy or level of acquaintance.

While the Bangla second person pronoun has three forms corresponding to levels of honorificity – *apni*, *tumi* and *tui* – the Ulti second person pronoun has only one form, *tumsi*; the level of honorificity in Ulti can only be discerned from the honorific agreement marker on the verb, not the pronoun itself, whereas in Bangla it can be discerned from both the pronoun and the agreement marker.

This example set looks at person and honorific agreement (in bold) in Ulti (i) and Bangla (ii), for: first, 8(a); second, 8(b–c), informal and intimate; third, persons 8(d), for a construction in simple present tense. This agreement pattern is consistent across all tenses and aspects in both Ulti and Bangla.

| | | | | | |
|---|---|---|---|---|---|
| 8 (a) | (i) | həmsi | kʰobrɑ | ʈɑk-**i** | (Ulti) |
| | (ii) | ɑmi | mɑŋʃo | kʰɑ-**i** | (Bangla) |
| | | 1PS | meat | eat.1P | |
| | | 'I eat meat.' | | | |
| (b) | (i) | t̪ʊmsi | kʰobrɑ | ʈɑk-**o** | (Ulti) |
| | (ii) | t̪umi | mɑŋʃo | ʈɑk-**o** | (Bangla) |
| | | 2PS | meat | eat.2P | |
| | | 'You (informal) eat meat.' | | | |
| (c) | (i) | t̪ʊmsi | kʰobrɑ | ʈɑk-**iʃ** | (Ulti) |
| | ii) | t̪ui | mɑŋʃo | ʈɑk-**iʃ** | (Bangla) |
| | | 2PS | meat | eat.2P | |
| | | 'You (intimate) eat meat.' | | | |
| (d) | (i) | ɪnsi/ʊnsi | kʰobrɑ | ʈɑk-**e** | (Ulti) |
| | (ii) | e/o | kʰobrɑ | ʈɑk-**e** | (Bangla) |
| | | 3PS | meat | eat.3P | |
| | | 'They (sg.) eat meat.' | | | |

Although *mashi* is described as a feminine gender marker, it is a semantic gender marker, not a grammatical one, so it does not participate in agreement.

## Tense, Aspect and Mood

Verbs in Ulti inflect for tense and aspect, as well as for causation, conjunctive participle marking and infinitival marking. All these markers come from Bangla, the reasons for which have been explained above. These are all inflectional morphemes; the only derivational process that some verbs in Ulti undergo is the nominalization process, when the suffix *-(u)nsi* attaches to them. This phenomenon will be discussed in detail later.

In the following example sets, we see the various tense and aspect markings (highlighted in bold) on the verb for first person singular in both Ulti (i) and Bangla (ii). This pattern, i.e. the order of morpheme attachment, is consistent throughout the language(s).

9 Simple Present/Habitual

| | | | | |
|---|---|---|---|---|
| (a) (i) | həmsi | kʰuʈni | kʰuʈ-**i** | (Ulti) |
| (ii) | ɑmi | kɔt̪ʰɑ | bol-**i** | (Bangla) |
| | 1PS | talk.N | talk.1P | |
| | 'I talk.' | | | |

Simple Past

| | | | | |
|---|---|---|---|---|
| (b) (i) | həmsi | kʰuʈni | kʰuʈ-**l**-ɑm | (Ulti) |
| (ii) | ɑmi | kɔt̪ʰɑ | bol-**l**-ɑm | (Bangla) |
| | 1PS | talk.N | talk.Pst.1P | |
| | 'I talked/spoke.' | | | |

Simple Future

| | | | | |
|---|---|---|---|---|
| (c) (i) | həmsi | kʰuʈni | kʰuʈ-**b**-o | (Ulti) |
| (ii) | ɑmi | kɔt̪ʰɑ | bol-**b**-o | (Bangla) |
| | 1PS | talk.N | talk.Fut.1P | |
| | 'I will talk.' | | | |

Present Progressive

| | | | | |
|---|---|---|---|---|
| (d) (i) | həmsi | kʰuʈni | kʰuʈ-**cʰ**-i | (Ulti) |
| (ii) | ɑmi | kɔt̪ʰɑ | bol-**cʰ**-i | (Bangla) |
| | 1PS | talk.N | talk.Pres.1P | |
| | 'I am talking.' | | | |

Present Perfect

| | | | | |
|---|---|---|---|---|
| (e) (i) | həmsi | kʰuʈni | kʰuʈ-**e**-**cʰ**-i | (Ulti) |
| (ii) | ɑmi | kɔt̪ʰɑ | bol-**e**-**cʰ**-i | (Bangla) |
| | 1PS | talk.N | talk.Pft.Pres.1P | |
| | 'I have spoken.' | | | |

Past Progressive

| | | | | |
|---|---|---|---|---|
| (f) (i) | həmsi | kʰuʈni | kʰuʈ-**cʰil**-ɑm | (Ulti) |
| (ii) | ɑmi | kɔt̪ʰɑ | bol-**cʰil**-ɑm | (Bangla) |
| | 1PS | talk.N | talk.Pst.1P | |
| | 'I was talking.' | | | |

Past Perfect

| | | | | |
|---|---|---|---|---|
| (g) (i) | həmsi | kʰuʈni | kʰuʈ-**e**-**cʰil**-ɑm | (Ulti) |
| (ii) | ɑmi | kɔt̪ʰɑ | bol-**e**-**cʰil**-ɑm | (Bangla) |
| | 1PS | talk.N | talk.Pft.Pst.1P | |
| | 'I had spoken.' | | | |

Past Habitual

| | | | | |
|---|---|---|---|---|
| (h) (i) | həmsi | kʰuʈni | kʰuʈ-t̪-ɑm | (Ulti) |
| (ii) | ɑmi | kɔt̪ʰɑ | bol-t̪-ɑm | (Bangla) |
| | 1PS | talk.N | talk.HabPst.1P | |
| | 'I used to talk.' | | | |

In simplex verbs in both Ulti (i) and Bangla (ii), the tense, aspect and agreement are marked on the verb.

| | | | | |
|---|---|---|---|---|
| 10 (a) (i) | t̪umsi-rɑ | pɔt̪-o | | (Ulti) |
| (ii) | t̪om-rɑ | pɔt̪-o | | (Bangla) |
| | 2P.PlCla | leave.2P | | |
| | 'You guys leave.' | | | |
| (b) (i) | həmsi | ʈɑkni | ʈek-e-cʰ-i | (Ulti) |
| (ii) | ɑmi | kʰɑbɑr | kʰe-e-cʰ-i | (Bangla) |
| | 1PS | food | eat.Pft.Pres.1P | |
| | 'I have eaten food.' | | | |

In complex verbs, it is usually the light verb that takes the inflections and agreement, irrespective of the source language or the composition of the complex verb: (N+V), (A+V) or (V+V) in 11(a), 11(b) or 11(c), respectively.

| | | | | | | | |
|---|---|---|---|---|---|---|---|
| 11 (a) (i) | həmsi | ʃiɽi | d̪ie | gɔɖɖor | mɑʃi | hoe | g-e-cʰ-i | (Ulti) |
| (ii) | ɑmi | ʃiɽi | die | pore | | | g-e-cʰ-i | (Bangla) |
| | 1PS | stairs | by | fall | | be | go.Pft.Pres.1P | |
| | 'I have fallen down the stairs.' | | | | | | | |

| | | | | | | |
|---|---|---|---|---|---|---|
| (b) (i) | t̪o-r | ʃɑt̪rɑ | bilɑ | hoe | g-ɛ-cʰ-e | (Ulti) |
| (ii) | t̪o-r | ʃɑɽi | nɔʃt̪o | hoe | g-ɛ-cʰ-e | (Bangla) |
| | 2PS.Gen | saree | bad | be | go.Pft.Pres.3P | |
| | 'Your saree has become damaged.' | | | | | |
| (c) (i) | ɟɔɟmɑn-rɑ | kot̪i-d̪er | ɑɽijɑl | bilɑ | kor-cʰ-e | (Ulti) |
| (ii) | loke-rɑ | kot̪i-d̪er | kʰub | ɔpomɑn | kor-cʰ-e | (Bangla) |
| | public.PlCla | koti.Pl.Gen | much | insult | do.Pres.3P | |
| | 'The people are insulting the kotis a lot.' | | | | | |

In serial verb constructions (d), the final verb takes the inflections and agrees with the subject.

| | | | | | | | | |
|---|---|---|---|---|---|---|---|---|
| (d) (i) | həmsi-r | ɑɟke | ʈɑnɑ | mɑʃi | fo | kort̪e | hɔ-b-e | (Ulti) |
| (ii) | ɑmɑ-r | ɑɟke | bʰuru | | | kort̪e | hɔ-b-e | (Bangla) |
| | 1PS.Gen | today | eyebrows | | trim | do | be.Fut.3P | |
| | 'I will have to shape my eyebrows today.' | | | | | | | |

Modals (highlighted in bold) in Ulti include the obligatory mood (12a), experiencer mood (12b), conditional (12c) and ability (12d). As can be seen from this example set, Ulti has no separate modal verbs of its own; it gets its modal verbs and verb roots from the ML Bangla.

| 12 (a) (i) | ʊnsi | ɟod̪i | pot̪t̪e | pɑre | t̪ɑhole | o-r | pɔt̪ɑ | **ucit̪** | (Ulti) |
|---|---|---|---|---|---|---|---|---|---|
| (ii) | o | ɟod̪i | ɑʃt̪e | pɑre | t̪ɑhole | o-r | ɑʃɑ | **ucit̪** | (Bangla) |
| | 3PS | if | come | can | then | 3PS.Gen | come | should | |

'If they can come, then they should come.'

| (b) (i) | ɑmɑ-r | ɟ$^{h}$orni | ɟuɽ-e | k$^{h}$ub | ciʃʃɑ | **lɑg**-c$^{h}$-e | (Ulti) |
|---|---|---|---|---|---|---|---|
| (ii) | ɑmɑ-r | gojnɑ | por-e | k$^{h}$ub | b$^{h}$ɑlo | **lɑg**-c$^{h}$-e | (Bangla) |
| | 1PS.Gen | jewellery | wear.Cpm | very | good | feel.Pres.3P | |

'I feel very good, wearing jewellery.'

| (c) (i) | ʃɑt̪rɑ | nɑ | ɟur-**le** | bɑd̪$^{h}$ɑi | mɑnɑ | ɟɑ-e | nɑ | (Ulti) |
|---|---|---|---|---|---|---|---|---|
| (ii) | ʃɑɽi | nɑ | por-**le** | bɑd̪$^{h}$ɑi | mɑnɑ | ɟɑ-e | nɑ | (Bangla) |
| | saree | Neg | wear.Cond | badhai | celebrate | go.Hab | Neg | |

'One cannot go for badhai if one does not wear a saree.'

| (d) (i) | ʊnsi | həmsi-r | kɔt̪$^{h}$ɑ | cɑmt̪e | **pɑr**-c$^{h}$-e | nɑ | (Ulti) |
|---|---|---|---|---|---|---|---|
| (ii) | o | ɑmɑ-r | kɔt̪$^{h}$ɑ | buɟ$^{h}$t̪e | **pɑr**-c$^{h}$-e | nɑ | (Bangla) |
| | 3PS | 1PS.Gen | talk | understand | can.Pres.3P | Neg | |

'They (sg.) cannot understand what I'm saying.'

*The Ulti suffix*

Most verbs in Ulti occur in free variation with their Bangla counterparts (if any). But there is a set of verbs in Ulti where, apart from the Bangla and Ulti alternations, the same verb root (highlighted in bold) can present itself in multiple forms but with essentially the same meaning:

| 13 (i) | həmsi/ɑmi | TV | d̪ek$^{h}$-c$^{h}$-i | |
|---|---|---|---|---|
| (ii) | həmsi/ɑmi | TV | **cɑm**-c$^{h}$-i | |
| (iii) | həmsi/ɑmi | TV | **cɑm**-ʊnsi | |
| (iv) | həmsi/ɑmi | TV | **cɑm**-ʊnsi | kor-c$^{h}$-i |
| | 1PS | TV | see.Pres.1P/see | do.Pres.1P |

'I am watching TV.'

This example set takes into account a present progressive construction. However, this range of variation in verbal forms is consistent across all tenses and aspects for this set of verbs. In example 13(i), the verb root *d̪ek$^{h}$-* is from Bangla, while in examples 13(ii–iv), the verb root *cam-* comes from bare Ulti. In 13(ii), as demonstrated throughout this chapter, the Ulti verb takes inflectional and agreement markers from Bangla. The pattern in 13(iv) is also predictable, with the light verb taking the inflectional and agreement markers. Which leaves us with two questions:

(a) What is the nature of the suffix *-ʊnsi* that attaches to the verb root *-cam* in 13(iii) and 13(iv)?
(b) Where are the inflectional and agreement markers in 13(iii) that would tell us how the event is anchored in time?

Before we address these questions, consider this:

| | | | | | | | |
|---|---|---|---|---|---|---|---|
| 14 | (i) * | həmsi | TV | cɑm-c$^{h}$-i | mɑʃi | | |
| | (ii) | həmsi | TV | | cɑm-ʊnsi | mɑʃi | |
| | (iii) * | həmsi | TV | | cɑm-ʊnsi | | kor-c$^{h}$-i mɑʃi |
| | (iv) ? | həmsi | TV | | cɑm-ʊnsi | mɑʃi | korc$^{h}$i |
| | | 1PS | TV | see.Pres.1P/ | see | | do.Pres.1P |
| | | 'I am watching TV.' | | | | | |

All these constructions carry the same meaning: 'I am watching TV'. Examples 13(i–iv) also mean the same. The constructions in 14(i) and 14(iii) are considered ungrammatical (* indicates ungrammaticality), while those in 14(ii) and 14(iv) are considered grammatical. However, 14(iv) is not a preferred usage for aesthetic reasons – it is considered too unwieldy (? indicates non-preference). Here we see that the inflected verbs cannot combine with *mashi*, but the verb + *ʊnsi* forms can, even when they are part of a complex verb construction. We have also seen that *mashi* combines almost exclusively with nominals. This leads us to argue that the verb + *ʊnsi* form is a nominal form, with the derivational suffix *-ʊnsi* acting as a nominalizer. This noun is then capable of combining with *mashi* to form a nominal compound. Schematically, it can be represented thus, where Nom is short for nominalizer:

| | | | | | | |
|---|---|---|---|---|---|---|
| (A) | Verb | + | -ʊnsi (Nom) | → | | noun |
| (B) | Noun | + | mɑʃi | → | mɑʃi | compound |

This *mashi* compound then acts as a single lemma that can be selected during language production in the same way as any other noun.

The next question is to do with examples 13(iii) and 14(ii), and how they are anchored as events in time. The speakers judge these forms, with no tense or aspectual information, to be the least preferred to use in a stand-alone sentence. The default reading of either of these sentences is that it is in the simple present or present progressive, i.e. the event is taking place at the time of utterance. But when modified with time adverbials or placed in a context which has already established the time frame, then these constructions can be used without any trouble. For instance, in the sentence 15(a), without the time adverbial, the meaning of the sentence is ambiguous with regard to the time and nature of the event. But with the time adverbial, the ambiguity is resolved. Further context provided by the discourse will clarify whether the sentence is supposed to be in progressive aspect or in perfect.

| 15 (a) | gɔt̪o | ʃapt̪ɑ-e | t̪ʊmsi-rɑ | gurumɑ-r | k$^{h}$ol-e | pɔt̪-onsi |
|---|---|---|---|---|---|---|
| | last | week.Loc | 2P.PlCla | guru.Gen | house.Loc | go |

'Last week you (pl.) went to Guruma's house.'

From these examples, it is apparent that the sentence can drop the tensed light verb (often the do-verb) when it follows the derived nominal that may or may not combine with *mashi*. This is a process that finds no equivalence in Bangla or with other nominal verbs in Ulti.

In 16(a), which is an Ulti construction, both constructions are grammatical because the main verb in the (N+V) construction is the derived nominal form with the *-ʊnsi* suffix, which allows the light verb to be dropped in (ii). In 16(b), the corresponding Bangla constructions show us that the light verb in Bangla cannot be dropped as it can in Ulti. In 16(c), we see that even in an Ulti (N+V) construction, the light verb cannot be dropped if the noun is not derived from the verb and ending in *-ʊnsi*.

| 16 (a) (i) | həmsi-r | mɑ | pɑk-ʊnsi | kor-e-c$^{h}$-e | | (Ulti) |
|---|---|---|---|---|---|---|
| (ii) | həmsi-r | mɑ | pɑk-ʊnsi | | | |
| | 1PS.Gen | mother | cook | do.Pft.Pres.3P | | |

'My mother has cooked.'

| (b) (i) | ɑmɑ-r | mɑ | rɑnnɑ | kor-e-c$^{h}$-e | | (Bangla) |
|---|---|---|---|---|---|---|
| (ii) * | ɑmɑ-r | mɑ | rɑnnɑ | | | |
| | 1PS.Gen | mother | cook | do.Pft.Pres.3P | | |

'My mother has cooked.'

| (c) (i) | mit̪ɑ | ʊnsi | t̪onnɑ-ke | k$^{h}$umur | kor-e-c$^{h}$-e | (Ulti) |
|---|---|---|---|---|---|---|
| (ii) * | mit̪ɑ | ʊnsi | t̪onnɑ-ke | k$^{h}$umur | | |
| | Mita | that | man.Dat | mouth | do.Pft.Pres.3P | |

'Mita has given that man an oral job.'

It is also noteworthy that the verb root *pak-* in 16(a) does not inflect for tense and aspect or agree with the subject in the manner of verb roots like *cam-* (e.g., *camc$^{h}$i*) or *kɔr-* (e.g., *korchi*), which come from Ulti and Bangla respectively. This is because *pak-* is a Hindi root verb meaning 'to cook' that is borrowed by Ulti speakers and nominalized in order to form a new

Ulti lexical item. This is also seen in the case of *gir-ʊnsi*, which contains the Hindi verb root *gir-* ('to fall'; 17-l in Table 4.2) and does not take the Bangla inflectional and agreement markers.

The presence of so many competing forms for each of these verbs brings into question the reasons behind their existence in the language, as it clearly violates the Ockham's razor principle[1] of linguistic economy. One way to explain this would be to look at Ulti as a language that is beginning to develop its own derivational affixes or system morphemes (*-ʊnsi*) for the purpose of forming new Ulti lexical items. This process is not very common but is productive in its ability to nominalize any verb from both Bangla and Ulti, and on rare occasions, even Hindi (17-k and 17-l). In some cases, the reason behind the process is to fill a gap in the language by adding an Ulti lexical item for an action, as in the case of examples 17(g) to 17(k), all of which have Hindi or Bangla verb roots and no Ulti counterparts. Example 17(l) exists despite having an Ulti counterpart, *goddor mashi hoe jaoa* ('to fall'), just like 17(a) to 17(e) exist despite having arguably simpler structural alternatives in the language that have Ulti as the root morpheme. In the words of the speakers, the *-ʊnsi* forms are considered more formal, more 'Ulti' forms of the verbs that are available in the language, and are indicative of, possibly, the nascent stages of the formation of a higher register in the language.

**Table 4.2** ***Derived -ʊnsi nominals***

| 17 | Derived -ʊnsi nominal | Verb root/ Noun | Meaning | Source language |
|---|---|---|---|---|
| (a) | cɑm-ʊnsi | cɑm- | to take in | Ulti |
| (b) | ʈɑk-ʊnsi | ʈɑk- | to eat | Ulti |
| (c) | pɔt̪-onsi | pɔt̪- | to leave | Ulti |
| (d) | ʈʰip-ʊnsi | ʈʰip- | to stay | Ulti |
| (e) | kʰuʈ-ʊnsi | kʰuʈ- | to talk | Ulti |
| (f) | nid̪r-ɑnsi | nid̪rɑ (N) | sleep | Bangla |
| (g) | lɑg-ʊnsi | lɑg- | to feel | Bangla |
| (h) | kɔr-onsi | kɔr- | to do | Bangla |
| (i) | ʊʈʰ-ʊnsi | ɔʈʰ- | to get up | Bangla |
| (j) | likʰ-ʊnsi | lekʰ- | to write | Bangla |
| (k) | pɑk-ʊnsi | pɑk- | to cook | Hindi |
| (l) | gir-ʊnsi | gir- | to fall | Hindi |

Example 17(f) is unique in that it is the only instance where the *-ʊnsi* suffix attaches to a noun, making it an inflectional process where the resultant noun *nid̪ransi* ('sleep') marks the formation of an Ulti noun from a Bangla one. It then participates in the Ulti complex verb in the same manner as *camʊnsi* ('to take in'), etc., do. Schematically, it can be represented thus (where Nom is short for nominalizer):

| (C) | nid̪rɑ | + | -ʊnsi | → | nid̪rɑnsi |
|---|---|---|---|---|---|
| | Bangla N | | (Nom) | | Ulti N |

The semantic implications of *mashi* forming a compound with these *-ʊnsi* forms will be discussed in detail in the next chapter.

## *Negation*

The negation marker *nathi* in Ulti is one of the rare features that demonstrates selectional restrictions in the language with respect to source language. In some cases it occurs in free variation with the Bangla negation marker *na*, while in others it occurs in complementary distribution with *na*.

In simple yes/no questions, both *na* and *nat̪ʰi* (highlighted in bold in all the subsequent examples) can be used to answer the question.

| 18 (a) | Q: | ɔɟɔj | ki | d̪illi | ɟɑbe? | ('Will Ajay go to Delhi?') |
|---|---|---|---|---|---|---|
| | A: | nɑ/**nɑt̪ʰi** | | | | ('No.') |

In case the answer is followed by a full sentence, we get the following possibilities:

| (b) | (i) | ɔɟɔj | d̪illi-t̪e | pɔt̪-onsi | mɑʃi | **nɑt̪ʰi** |
|---|---|---|---|---|---|---|
| | (ii) ?? | ɔɟɔj | d̪illi-t̪e | pɔt̪-onsi | mɑʃi | nɑ |
| | (iii) ?? | ɔɟɔj | d̪illi-t̪e | ɟɑ-b-e | | **nɑt̪ʰi** |
| | (iv) | ɔɟɔj | d̪illi-t̪e | ɟɑ-b-e | | nɑ |
| | | Ajay | Delhi.Loc | go | | Neg |
| | | 'Ajay will not go to Delhi.' | | | | |

Here, we see that the Ulti negation marker appears with the Ulti lexical root, while the Bangla negation marker appears with the Bangla verb. The other alternatives, where the Bangla verb appears with the Ulti negation and vice-versa, are strongly dispreferred in this case (indicated by ??).

When the predicate is an Ulti adjective (c), we find that both *na* and *nat̪ʰi* 18(c-i) to 18(c-ii), can negate it. However, the Ulti negation marker does not appear with a Bangla adjective 18(c-iii). The Bangla negation marker is shown with the Bangla adjective, as in 18(c-iv).

| | | | | |
|---|---|---|---|---|
| (c) (i) | ʊnsi | t̪onnɑ-t̪ɑ | ciʃʃɑ | **nɑt̪ʰi** |
| (ii) | ʊnsi | t̪onnɑ-t̪ɑ | ciʃʃɑ | nɑ |
| (iii) * | ʊnsi | t̪onnɑ-t̪ɑ | bʰɑlo | **nɑt̪ʰi** |
| (iv) | ʊnsi | t̪onnɑ-t̪ɑ | bʰɑlo | nɑ |
| | that | man.Cla | good | Neg |
| | 'That man is not good.' | | | |

In equative constructions, both *na* and *nat̪ʰi* can act as the negative copula in present tense constructions 18(d–e). However, in past tense (18f) and future tense (18g) constructions, we see that *nat̪ʰi* can only be selected if the predicate contains no tensed verb, and has either nominals or adjectives. This is also corroborated by examples 18(b–c). In example 18(g), we see that in order to select *nat̪ʰi*, the tensed verb *ho-* is nominalized into its corresponding *-ʊnsi* form. This example also demonstrates how negation in Ulti violates the Morpheme Order Principle for code-switching that the MLF is based on.

| | | | | |
|---|---|---|---|---|
| (d) (i) | ʊnsi | hɘmsi-r | sʊɖɖʰɑ | **nɑt̪ʰi** |
| (ii) | ʊnsi | hɘmsi-r | sʊɖɖʰɑ | nɑ |
| | 3PS | 1PS.Gen | father | Neg |
| | 'He is not my father.' | | | |

| | | | |
|---|---|---|---|
| (e) (i) | ɔɟɔj | bilɑ | **nɑt̪ʰi** |
| (ii) | ɔɟɔj | bilɑ | nɑ |
| | Ajay | bad | Neg |
| | 'Ajay is not bad.' | | |

| | | | | | |
|---|---|---|---|---|---|
| (f) (i) | Razia | ciʃʃɑ | nihɑrin | | **nɑt̪ʰi** |
| (ii) | Razia | ciʃʃɑ | nihɑrin | cʰilo | nɑ |
| | Razia | good | girl | be.Pst.3P | Neg |
| | 'Razia was not a good girl.' | | | | |

| | | | | | |
|---|---|---|---|---|---|
| (g) (i) | bɑni | nɑek | **nɑt̪ʰi** | hɔ-ʊnsi | |
| (ii) | bɑni | nɑek | | hɔ-b-e | nɑ |
| | Bani | area head | Neg | be/be.Fut.3P | Neg |
| | 'Bani will not be a *naek*.' | | | | |

For all tense and aspect markers the verb is negated by *na*, except in a few exceptions, as shown in 19(a-i) to 19(a-ii), 19(b-i) and 19(c-i). Here we see that when the sentence has a tensed final verb, it is negated with *na* 19(a-iii), 19(b-ii), 19(c-ii). However, as seen in the previous examples, if in the predicate of the sentence the tensed final verb has been dropped so that it now possesses only nouns, adjectives or noun phrases, then it is negated by *nat̪ʰi*.

| 19 (a) (i) | həmsi | cʰɔlla | maʃi | | **nat̪ʰi** |
|---|---|---|---|---|---|
| (ii) | həmsi | cʰɔlla | | kɔr-onsi | **nat̪ʰi** |
| (iii) | həmsi | cʰɔlla | | kor-t̪-am | na |
| | 1PS | beg | | do/do.PstHab.1P | Neg |

'I never used to beg for a living.'

| (b) (i) | ɔɟoj | ʈakni | **nat̪ʰi** | ʈak-ʊnsi | |
|---|---|---|---|---|---|
| (ii) | ɔɟɔj | ʈakni | | ʈak-b-e | na |
| | Ajay | food | Neg | eat/eat.Fut.3P | Neg |

'Ajay will not eat food.'

| (c) (i) | həmsi | aʈijal | kʰuʈni | **nat̪ʰi** | |
|---|---|---|---|---|---|
| (ii) | həmsi | aʈijal | kʰuʈni | kʰuʈ-i | na |
| | 1PS | much | talk.N | talk.1P | Neg |

'I don't talk very much.'

From these examples, we see that *nat̪ʰi* can occur both before and after the constituent it is negating. While it comes after most other nouns and adjectives, when it comes to nouns ending with *-ʊnsi*, the surface realization can have *nat̪ʰi* both before and after the constituent, as in examples 20(a-i) to 20(a-ii). Speaker judgement on the grammaticality and acceptability of these constructions varies wildly, so it is difficult to determine which construction is default and which is marked, if any.

| 20 (a) (i) | həmsi | sʊɖɖʰi-ke | ɟʰɔlka | **nat̪ʰi** | cam-ʊnsi | |
|---|---|---|---|---|---|---|
| (ii) | həmsi | sʊɖɖʰi-ke | ɟʰɔlka | | cam-ʊnsi | **nat̪ʰi** |
| (iii) | həmsi | sʊɖɖʰi-ke | ɟʰɔlka | | cam-a-i | ni |
| | 1PS | mother.Dat | money | Neg | take/take.Caus.1P | Neg |

'I have not given money to my mother.'

In every other instance where a tensed verb occurs, like modal, conditional, imperative, interrogative, infinitival (with emphatic marker), neither–nor, relative and NPI constructions, *na* is selected to negate the constituent/proposition.

The question to be considered, then, is: does *nathi* carry any tense and aspect features? Looking at the equative constructions, it seems apparent that *nathi* is a copula just like *na*. Speakers of Ulti say that in any non-equative construction, *nathi* does not convey any information as to the time or aspectual nature of the event. That has to be added into the discourse with the help of a time adverbial or other context clues. In effect, *nathi* does not add any layer of meaning or information to the sentence other than negation. While *nathi* does not appear with tensed verbs in a sentence, it does negate events in an ambiguous way when it appears alongside an *-unsi* nominal. Why it behaves the way it does is something that would require further research and a deeper understanding of the syntactic processes at play in Ulti.[2]

## A Conversation in Ulti

Given below is an excerpt from a conversation in Ulti which demonstrates most of the features discussed in this chapter in discourse. The interlocutors are Sheila (S), Madhu (M), Nina (N) and Hema (H); they are discussing the possible reasons for the apparent increase in size of Madhu's breasts. The italicized lines are spoken in Ulti, while the unitalicized lines show the corresponding sentences in Bangla. The constituents in square brackets demonstrate Bangla counterparts for the Ulti constituents in bold type.

Excerpt 3

S: *Tor* ***dharki mashi*** *ta* ***ariyal cissa*** *lagche to. Already kintu* ***dharki*** *ta dekh . . .*

S: Tor [buk] ta [khub bhalo] lagche to. Already kintu [buk] ta dekh . . .

M: ***Jog mashi fo*** *korechi na . . .*

M: [Chul] [ketechi] na . . .

N: *Ei,* ***tumsi dharki mashir tabli mashi*** *na ki emni* ***khauri****?*

N: Ei, [tomar buker surgery (hoyeche)] na ki emni [nokol]?

M: *Original.*

M: Original.

N: *Original? Amar* ***khole*** *aajke* ***khutchilo niharin*** *ra, ki* ***unsir dharki ariyal*** *keno hoye geche. . . .*

N: Original? Amar [barite] aajke [bolchilo] [mohila] ra, ki [or buk boro] keno hoye geche . . .

H: ***Dharki*** *ta* ***ariyal*** *hoyeche . . .*

H: [Buk] ta [bishal] hoyeche . . .

N: ***Humsir suddhi khutchilo*** *janish . . . je* ***unsir dharki*** *gulo* ***ariyal*** *. . .*

N: [Amar ma] [bolchilo] janish . . . je [or buk] gulo [bishal] . . .

M: *Tai? Kokhon?*

M: Tai? Kokhon?

N: *Ei aajke. Ami abar amar* ***suddhi*** *ke* ***camalam****, tomar je bacca . . .* (laughs) *bacca jeno . . .*

N: Ei aajke. Ami abar amar [ma] ke [bojhalam], tomar je bacca . . . (laughs) bacca jeno . . .

H: *Ki* ***bila****, chhi . . . (laughs)*

H: Ki [baje], chhi . . . (laughs)

N: *. . . na ashe oi oushudh khay ei beti tar jonno* ***ariyal*** *. . .*

N: . . . na ashe oi oushudh khay ei beti tar jonno [boro] . . .
S: ***Taepka tepki*** *jeno na hoy er jonno. Na or* ***tattoo mashi*** *ta* ***cissa*** *hoyeche bol* ***dharki*** *te?*
S: [Chhele meye] jeno na hoy er jonno. Na or [tattoo] ta [shundor] hoyeche bol [buk]e?
H: *Hya . . . tattoo ta shundor . . .*
H: Hya . . . tattoo ta shundor . . .

Translation

S: Your breasts are looking very good. The breasts are already . . . look . . .
M: It's because I got a haircut . . .
N: Hey, did you get your breasts surgically done (on the surgical table) or is it just fake?
M: Original.
N: Original? The women in my house were talking about it today, that why have her breasts gotten so big . . .
H: The breasts have become huge . . .
N: My mother was saying, you know . . . that her breasts are huge . . .
M: Really? When?
N: Just today. So, I explained to my mother, your child . . . (laughs). So that you don't . . .
H: So bad, chhi . . .
N: . . . have a child, this girl has those medicines that's why they are big . . .
S: So that she has no children. But don't you think her tattoo on her breasts look beautiful?
H: Yes . . . the tattoo is beautiful . . .

## Conclusion

While working on a language like Ulti, it must be kept in mind that since it is acquired as a second language by people from various linguistic backgrounds and spoken across the subcontinent, one of the possible ways to understand its structure would be to look at the languages in contact with the speakers of Ulti, and to examine the other forms of hijra languages and the code-switching patterns they display. While the patterns of code-switching in Ulti largely coincide with the observations made by Myers-Scotton in the MLF and 4-M models, the behaviour of *nathi* in the way it occurs both before and after the *-unsi* constituent invites us to consider whether the structure of Ulti might not be as simple as first presumed.

This chapter examines the nature of code-switching in Ulti, and provides an insight into its structure and grammar. It opens up the scope to continue research in Ulti and its many other varieties from a structural perspective, and tries to understand the relationship between the social and linguistic background of the speakers and their motivations as a speech community, and how these aspects manifest themselves through structural forms and lexical choices in a language. This question will be further explored in the next chapter, which deals with *mashi* and the question of gender in Ulti.

## Notes

1 Ockham's razor (also spelled Occam's razor) is a principle stated by the scholastic philosopher William of Ockham (1285–1347/49) that *pluralitas non est ponenda sine necessitate*, i.e. 'plurality should not be posited without necessity.' The principle gives precedence to simplicity: of two competing theories, the simpler explanation of an entity is to be preferred. See https://www.britannica.com/topic/Occams-razor, accessed 6 April 2023.

2 In a multilingual environment where lexical items are borrowed from various languages and used in one sentence, it becomes necessary to consider whether Ulti might not also be an amalgam of linguistic structures not just from Bangla, but from other languages the speakers are in contact with, like Hindi and the various regional varieties spoken in Bengal. The influence of Hindi might be one possible way of explaining why *nathi* appears before the derived nominal in its surface realization in Ulti; Hindi demonstrates pre-verbal and pre-adjectival negation that is absent in Bangla.

# 5

# Gendering Ulti

## What is *Mashi*?

As we have seen in the previous chapter, the grammar of Ulti closely resembles that of Bangla. Hence, like Bangla, Ulti possesses no grammatical gender and consequently, no gender agreement. Yet, Ulti has gender as it is a feature its speakers want to emphasize through their language as an expression of their gender identity. This chapter takes a deep look at what constitutes gender in Ulti, and examines the features and roles of the symbolic gender marker for feminine, *mashi,* in the Ulti language. In the first section, we reflect on what constitutes hijra-koti speech. In the second section, we explore the noun *mashi* and its various types in Ulti: kinship, obligatory and optional *mashi.*

### What Constitutes Hijra-Koti Speech?

In the previous chapters we looked at the lexical items in bare Ulti and how they embed themselves in the Bangla grammatical framework to form Ulti constructions. This leads us to consider the question: What constitutes an utterance in Ulti? And, by extension, what constitutes hijra-koti speech? Do they have the same characteristics as any other language?

Hall (2002), in her linguistic ethnography of Benaras hijras, differentiates *zanana boli* (feminine speech) from *mardana boli* (masculine speech), and identifies the former as 'a critical component of [the] second gender socialization process' of hijras and thereby their preferred form of speech (Hall 2002: 147). She describes the two *boli*s thus:

> The precise definition of these two terms varies . . . but members generally agree

> that *mardana boli* involves direct speech, 'stronger' curses, and masculine first-person verb forms, while *zanana boli* entails indirect speech (and is therefore deemed more polite), 'weaker' curses, and feminine first-person verb forms. Whether or not these qualities play out in the ordinary speech of non-hijra men and women has not yet been studied, but the hijras are no doubt identifying stereotypical perceptions of masculine and feminine behaviours in dominant north Indian culture . . . accept these distinctions as fact, and use them to instruct each other on how to build a 'less masculine' gender presentation. (Ibid.)

In linguistic terms, these shifts take place in the context of the variety of Hindi spoken in Benaras, where Hall conducted this study. Similar observations were made by Hall (2005) and Nagar (2008) in the context of the Hindi spoken by hijras in Delhi and Lucknow, respectively, where the speakers manipulate the grammatical gender system of Hindi to index their own subject position and gender identity vis-à-vis the society they live in. A koti or a hijra, before joining the community, would be socialized as a masculine person and employ masculine gender agreement for the first person in their speech to coindex their natural gender. However, when they interact with the community and/or perform their feminine personae, they would employ feminine gender agreement for the first person as well as for the other hijras and kotis they address or reference (in the second or third person). The only exception would be the use of masculine gender markers for reported speech while referencing their past/masculine identities, to distance themselves from a revered or reviled hijra or koti, and to express anger and aggression.

In example 1(a), the speaker is a hijra self-referencing herself in the present; hence, she uses feminine gender agreement on the verb. In example 1(b), a hijra is referring to the past selves of hijras who lived under a masculine identity in their natal homes; hence, the main and light verbs agree for masculine gender.

| | | | | | | |
|---|---|---|---|---|---|---|
| 1 | (a) | mæ | ɔrət̪ | ɟæsi | bolt̪-i | hu |
| | | 1PS | woman | like | speak.F | be.1PS |
| | | 'I speak like a woman.' | | | | |
| | (b) | g$^{h}$ər-me | t̪o | mərdɑnɑ | reht̪-e | t̪$^{h}$e |
| | | house.Loc | Top | masculine | stay.M | be.Pst.MPl |
| | | 'They'd live as men in the house.' | | | | |

These shifts in gender agreement in one's speech to index one's gender identity and community affiliation are a hallmark of hijra speech in the Hindi-speaking regions of the subcontinent. It is noteworthy that these constructions do not require the inclusion of Farasi lexical items to index hijra speech.

Similarly, in Bengal, the use of Ulti lexical items is not the only way to index hijra-koti speech. However, this is where the similarity ends. Bangla has no grammatical gender and does not participate in gender agreement, which makes it impossible for speakers to make the kind of gendered shifts in Bangla that they consciously do in Hindi. In the absence of a readymade linguistic system that performs the task that is so seminal to the identity construction of a hijra or a koti, i.e. to index their gender, the speakers of Ulti have developed their own system to perform the task.

The Bangla kinship term *mashi* (lit. 'maternal aunt') has been borrowed by speakers of Ulti and semantically extended so that it combines with nouns, pronouns and demonstratives to form compounds that carry a symbolic (feminine) gender feature. Since *mashi* (as used in Bangla) carries a strong semantic gender feature, the initial analysis of the Ulti data was conducted based on the assumption that *mashi* carries a (perhaps weaker) semantic gender feature in Ulti as well. In this chapter, I demonstrate the analytical steps by which I arrived at the conclusion that the best way to characterize *mashi* in Ulti is in terms of a symbolic gender feature. An initial look at the Ulti data indicated that since, as assumed, *mashi* carries a semantic gender feature, the nouns that form a compound with *mashi* do not alter the syntax of the language; they merely feminize the nouns – and, by extension, the language – at a semantic level, thereby symbolically indexing the desire of the speakers to identify as feminine/femme through their language in a world that is designed to systematically marginalize and stigmatize them for exercising their choice to present and identify as their chosen gender(s): (trans)femme/feminine.

As in the case of Hindi, hijra-koti speech can be indexed in Bangla without the inclusion of Ulti lexical items with the help of the term *mashi*, which can combine with lexical items in Bangla, Hindi and English as well as Ulti. Therefore, the following sentences, which include no Ulti lexical item, can constitute Ulti speech just because there is a minimum of one *mashi* compound in the sentence. In the following, examples (i) are in Ulti and (ii) are the Bangla counterparts of the same sentences. The *mashi* compounds are created in these contexts by combining *mashi* with the relevant Bangla lexical item.

| | | | | | | |
|---|---|---|---|---|---|---|
| 2 (a) (i) | ɑmɑ-r | **gɑɖi mɑʃi-**ʈɑ | kɑɟ | korc$^{h}$e | nɑ | (Ulti) |
| (ii) | ɑmɑ-r | gɑɖi-ʈɑ | kɑɟ | korc$^{h}$e | nɑ | (Bangla) |
| | 1PS.Gen | car.Cla | work | do | Neg | |
| | 'My car is not working.' | | | | | |

| | | | | | |
|---|---|---|---|---|---|
| (b) (i) | ɑmɑ-ke | **ɟɔl mɑʃi**-ʈɑ | d̪ɑ-o | t̪o | (Ulti) |
| (ii) | ɑmɑ-ke | ɟɔl-ʈɑ | d̪ɑ-o | t̪o | (Bangla) |
| | 1PS.Dat | water.Cla | give.2P | Top | |
| | 'Please give me the water.' | | | | |

*Mashi* and its various characteristics are discussed in detail below.

## Marking Gender as a Linguistic Feature in Ulti

Ulti, as mentioned above, has no grammatical gender. However, Ulti has a few nouns that do overtly mark natural gender. In the examples below, we see that the suffix *-a* on the noun marks masculine gender and the suffix *-i* feminine gender.

| | | | |
|---|---|---|---|
| 3 | (a) | sʊɖɖʰ-ɑ/sʊɖɖʰ-i | old man/woman |
| | (b) | ʈæpk-ɑ/ʈepk-i | boy/girl |
| | (c) | ʈonn-ɑ/ʈunn-i | man/woman |

It is noteworthy that all these nouns are meant to refer to cisgender people; there are no terms referring to hijra or koti identities that display a binary gender distinction morphologically as the terms above do. One of the reasons for this could be that most hijra or koti identities are not constructed on a gender binary framework; therefore, the question of such distinctions does not arise in the first place. Another reason is that whenever an identity *is* constructed in opposition to another along gender lines, such as *koti/panthi* ('koti'/'male lover') or *koti/parik* ('koti'/'male lover') or *tonna/laharan* ('cis man'/'cis woman'), the gender distinction is marked lexically instead of morphologically.

Nouns in Ulti can often combine with the noun *mashi* to form compound nouns that may or may not have the same meaning as the original noun. *Mashi* does not combine with larger noun phrases, though; it only combines with bare nouns, pronouns and demonstratives, as evident in the examples below. Further, as can be observed from examples 4(c) to 4(h), a case marker or a classifier can attach to a *mashi* compound, but *mashi* cannot be attached to a noun which has already been assigned case or has a classifier attached to it.

| | | | | | |
|---|---|---|---|---|---|
| 4 (a) | [ɪnsi] | mɑʃi | kɑlke | d̪ɔmd̪ɔm | pot̪-b-e |
| | 3PS | mashi | tomorrow | Dumdum | go.Fut.3P |
| | 'They (sg.) will go to Dumdum tomorrow.' | | | | |

| (b)* | [ɪnsi-r | bʰɑi-er | cʰele] | mɑʃi | kɑlke | d̪ɔmd̪ɔm | pot̪-b-e |
|---|---|---|---|---|---|---|---|
| | 3PS.Gen | brother.Gen | son | mashi | tomorrow | Dumdum | go.Fut.3P |

'Their(sg.) brother's son will go to Dumdum tomorrow.'

Here we see that while *mashi* can combine with the pronoun in 4(a), it cannot combine with an entire noun phrase, as shown in 4(b).

| (c) | həmsi | [[ɪnsi] | mɑʃi]-te | kɑl | d̪ɔmd̪ɔm | pot̪-b-o |
|---|---|---|---|---|---|---|
| | 1PS | this | mashi.Loc | tomorrow | Dumdum | go.Fut.1P |

'I will go to Dumdum tomorrow in this (car).'

| (d)* | həmsi | [[ɪnsi]-t̪e] | mɑʃi | kɑl | d̪ɔmd̪ɔm | pot̪-b-o |
|---|---|---|---|---|---|---|
| | 1PS | this.Loc | mashi | tomorrow | Dumdum | go.Fut.1P |

'I will go to Dumdum tomorrow in this (car).'

In example 4(c) we see that the *mashi* compound can be assigned a case marker, but a noun or pronoun that has already been assigned case cannot combine with *mashi*, as shown in 4(d).

| (e) | [[t̪æpkɑ] | mɑʃi]-t̪ɑ | həmsi-r | ʃɑt̪rɑ | bilɑ | kore | d̪i-l-o |
|---|---|---|---|---|---|---|---|
| | boy | mashi Cla | 1PS.Gen | clothes | dirty | do | give.Pft.3P |

'The boy has soiled my clothes.'

| (f)* | [t̪æpkɑ-t̪ɑ] | mɑʃi | həmsi-r | ʃɑt̪rɑ | bilɑ | kore | d̪i-l-o |
|---|---|---|---|---|---|---|---|
| | boy.Cla | mashi | 1PS.Gen | clothes | dirty | do | give.Pft.3P |

'The boy has soiled my clothes.'

In 4(e) we see that a classifier can attach itself to a *mashi* compound, but *mashi* cannot form a compound with a noun that already has a classifier attached to it, as shown in 4(f).

| (g) | [[t̪æpkɑ] | mɑʃi]-t̪ɑ-ke | t̪ɑkni | t̪ɑk-ɑ-o |
|---|---|---|---|---|
| | boy | mashi.Cla.Dat | food | eat.Caus.2P |

'Feed the boy.'

| (h)* | [t̪æpkɑ-t̪ɑ-ke] | mɑʃi | t̪ɑkni | t̪ɑk-ɑ-o |
|---|---|---|---|---|
| | boy.Cla.Dat | mashi | food | eat.Caus.2P |

'Feed the boy.'

In 4(g) and 4(h), we see a combination of 4(c) to 4(f), where *mashi* cannot combine with a noun when both classifiers and case markers are attached to it; it can only combine with a bare noun. This demonstrates that a *mashi* compound is a nominal compound which behaves in the same way as a bare noun would in Ulti.

*Mashi* is sensitive to noun classes in the language that behave differently in the way they combine with *mashi*. There are three types of *mashi* in the language: kinship *mashi*, obligatory *mashi* and optional *mashi*, each of which I discuss below.

### *Kinship Mashi*

The term *mashi* was borrowed into Ulti from Bangla, where it is used as a kinship term for 'aunt' (specifically, 'mother's sister'). In Bangla, it is also used to refer to and address older women who are not related to the speaker by blood. In the following examples, we see *mashi* combining with a feminine proper noun (5a), a masculine proper noun (5b), a common noun assigned genitive case that indicates the profession of the subject *mashi* (5c), and an inflectional noun that also indicates the profession of the subject (5d). All of these constructions create noun phrases where *mashi* refers to a person whose natural gender is assumed to be feminine.

**Table 5.1** ***Kinship mashi***

| 5 | Compound | Analysis | Meaning |
|---|---|---|---|
| | (a) ʃobʰa mɑʃi | noun {Shobha_F} + mashi | Shobha(F) aunty (+ANIM) |
| | (b) *rɑɟib mɑʃi | *noun {Rajib_M} + mashi | *Rajib(M) aunty (+ANIM) |
| | (c) kɑɟ-er mɑʃi | noun.Gen {work.Gen_F} + mashi | work.Gen aunty/maid(F) (+ANIM) |
| | (d) d̪ud̪ʰ-ali mɑʃi | noun {milkmaid_F} + mashi | the milkmaid(f) (+ANIM) |

This *mashi* has a semantic gender feature with the value [feminine] and selects only animate nouns that have feminine natural gender (both proper and common nouns). It can also occur independently, but only if its referent is a proper or common noun with feminine natural gender. It does not combine with any other kind of noun.

### *Obligatory Mashi*

In this case, *mashi* combines obligatorily with a noun to give us a compound noun. The nouns selected by obligatory *mashi* are not restricted by conditions of animacy, natural or grammatical gender, or source language. Examples include:

**Table 5.2** ***Obligatory mashi 1***

| 6 | Compound | Analysis | Meaning |
|---|---|---|---|
| (a) | kɔrmo mɑʃi | noun {work} + mashi | work (−ANIM) |
| (b) | ogni mɑʃi | noun {fire} + mashi | fire (−ANIM) |
| (c) | d̪ɔnt̪o mɑʃi | noun {tooth} + mashi | tooth (−ANIM) |
| (d) | ɑkʰija mɑʃi | noun {eyes} + mashi | eyes (−ANIM) |
| (e) | bɔgol mɑʃi | noun {side} + mashi | side (−ANIM) / neighbour (+ANIM) |

In these cases, the formal or archaic forms of Bangla nouns (N1s) combine with *mashi* to form Ulti compound nouns (N2s). These N1s would never be used independently of *mashi* in Ulti, despite the fact that Ulti heavily borrows lexical items from Bangla.

**Table 5.3** ***Obligatory mashi 2***

| 7 | Compound | Analysis | Meaning |
|---|---|---|---|
| (a) | d̪ʰonnu mɑʃi | noun {___} + mashi | earring −ANIM) |
| (b) | furfuri mɑʃi | noun {___} + mashi | smile (−ANIM) |
| (c) | gɔɖɖor mɑʃi | noun {___} + mashi | fallen (N) (−ANIM) |

In these cases, it is unclear where the N1s come from or what they mean independently of *mashi* in any other language/context, but in Ulti these N1s have meaning only when they are combined with *mashi.*

**Table 5.4** ***Obligatory mashi 3***

| 8 | Compound | Analysis | Meaning |
|---|---|---|---|
| (a) | bid̪d̪ɑ mɑʃi | noun {wisdom} + mashi | education (−ANIM) |
| (b) | kurkur mɑʃi | noun {cold} + mashi | refrigerator (−ANIM) |
| (c) | moɟɑ mɑʃi | noun {sock/condom} + mashi | condom (−ANIM) |
| (d) | gʰeugʰeu mɑʃi | noun {barking sound} + mashi | dog (+ANIM) |
| (e) | ɖʰipi mɑʃi | noun {low hills} + mashi | eyes (−ANIM) |
| (f) | pɑt̪ija mɑʃi | noun {ticket} + mashi | ticket collector (+ANIM) |
| (g) | ʈɑnɑ mɑʃi | noun {straight} + mashi | eyebrows (−ANIM) |
| (h) | ʃɑd̪ɑ mɑʃi | noun {white} + mashi | powder/ anything white (+/−ANIM) |
| (i) | lɑl mɑʃi | noun {red} + mashi | lipstick/periods/anything red (+/−ANIM) |
| (j) | ʈunʈuni mɑʃi | noun {ringtone} + mashi | phone (−ANIM) |

Here, we see that *mashi* combines with a noun (N1) to give us a new noun (N2) that is semantically distinct from N1. This derivation process can schematically be represented thus:

N1 + mashi → N2

where N2 can be interpreted as 'the thing that N1 gives (a) / makes (b) and (d) / looks like (c), (e) and (g) / sounds like (j) / relates to (f), (h) and (i)'.

It must be noted here that the N1s in this set of examples may or may not appear in the language independent of *mashi*, but those N1s will never carry the same meaning in Ulti as their corresponding N2s. In that respect, it is obligatory for *mashi* to combine with those nouns in order to give them a new meaning with denotations specific to the Ulti lexicon.

**Table 5.5 *Obligatory mashi 4***

| 9 | Compound | Analysis | Meaning |
|---|---|---|---|
| (a) | ɟindɑ mɑʃi | noun {alive} + mashi | alive (−ANIM) |
| (b) | hɛlo mɑʃi | noun {hello} + mashi | phone (−ANIM) |
| (c) | wɔt̪ər mɑʃi | noun {water} + mashi | water (−ANIM) |
| (d) | t̪əbijət̪ mɑʃi | noun {health} + mashi | health (−ANIM) |
| (e) | d̪unijɑ mɑʃi | noun {world} + mashi | world (−ANIM) |

Here, we see that when N1s are borrowed from Hindi/Urdu or English into Ulti, they combine with *mashi* to form Ulti N2s. The process is similar to the one taking place in example 6 for all the examples listed above except 9(b), which follows a derivational process similar to example 8. While it is possible for the N1s in this list to appear independently of *mashi*, as they do in their source languages, they will rarely – if at all – be used in these forms in an Ulti sentence. They need to be combined with *mashi* to be considered as Ulti lexical items that can be used felicitously in an Ulti sentence.

From all these cases, we can conclude that the purpose of the obligatory *mashi* is to coin new lexical items for the Ulti lexicon.

### *Optional Mashi*

In this case, *mashi* combines optionally with nouns to create an N2 not semantically distinct from its corresponding N1. The optional *mashi* is the most commonly occuring *mashi* in the language and combines with nouns very productively (barring a few exceptions, which we will discuss presently). Examples include:

**Table 5.6** ***Optional mashi 1***

| 10 | Compound | Analysis | Meaning |
|---|---|---|---|
| (a) | TV maʃi | noun {TV} + mashi | TV (−ANIM) |
| (b) | ɟɔl maʃi/pɑni maʃi/ wɔʈər maʃi | noun {water} + mashi | water (−ANIM) |
| (c) | kʰol maʃi | noun {house} + mashi | house (−ANIM) |
| (d) | kʰolʃɑ maʃi | noun {egg} + mashi | egg (−ANIM) |
| (e) | d̪ɔrpon maʃi/ʃiʃɑ maʃi/aenɑ maʃi | noun {mirror} + mashi | mirror (−ANIM) |
| (f) | kɔl maʃi | noun {tap} + mashi | tap (−ANIM) |
| (g) | roɖ maʃi | noun {road} + mashi | road (−ANIM) |
| (h) | dɔrʃon maʃi | noun {beard/body hair} + mashi | beard/body hair (−ANIM) |
| (i) | lɑhɑrɑn maʃi | noun {cis woman_F} + mashi | cis woman(f) (+ANIM) |
| (j) | ɟɔɟmɑn maʃi | noun {client¬s} + mashi | clients (+ANIM) |
| (k) | bæbʃɑ maʃi | noun {business} + mashi | business (−ANIM) |
| (l) | bɑkur maʃi | noun {theft} + mashi | theft (−ANIM) |
| (m) | bɔrkɑ piʈ maʃi | noun {older sibling} + mashi | older sibling (+ANIM) |
| (n) | ʈæpkɑ maʃi | noun {boy_M} + mashi | boy(m) (+ANIM) |
| (o) | ʃɑʈ̪rɑ maʃi | noun {clothes/saree}+ mashi | clothes/saree (−ANIM) |
| (p) | ɟog maʃi | noun {hair} + mashi | hair (−ANIM) |

From the examples above, one can say that optional *mashi* combines with words irrespective of their source language (10b), animacy and natural gender.

Apart from bare nouns, *mashi* also combines with pronouns (11e–h), demonstratives (11g–h), nouns of direction that constitute PPs (11a–d), and nominal forms of verbs that constitute part of (N+V) complex verbs (11i–j), but within certain constraints (that will be expanded upon later). Examples include:

**Table 5.7** ***Optional mashi 2***

| 11 | Compound | Analysis | Meaning |
|---|---|---|---|
| (a) | ɑg maʃi | noun {front} + mashi | front (−ANIM) |
| (b) | pi:cʰ maʃi | noun {behind} + mashi | behind (−ANIM) |
| (c) | ni:c maʃi | noun {below} + mashi | below (−ANIM) |

| | | |
|---|---|---|
| (d) upor maʃi | noun {above} + mashi | above (−ANIM) |
| (e) həmsi maʃi | pronoun {I_SG} + mashi | I (+ANIM) |
| (f) t̪ʊmsi maʃi | pronoun {you_SG} + mashi | you (+ANIM) |
| (g) ɪnsi maʃi | pronoun {they_SG_prox} + mashi | They(sg)(prox) (+ANIM) |
| (h) ʊnsi maʃi | pronoun {they_SG_dist} + mashi | They(sg)(dist) (+ANIM) |
| (i) ɪnsi maʃi | dem {this_prox} + mashi | This(prox) (−ANIM) |
| (j) ʊnsi maʃi | dem {that_dist} + mashi | That(dist) (−ANIM) |
| (k) camunsi maʃi | noun {take in} + mashi | Take in (n) (−ANIM) |
| (l) ʈakunsi maʃi | noun {eat} + mashi | Eat (n) (−ANIM) |

Of these, the *mashi* in 11(a–d) is obligatory, while the ones in 11(e–l) are optional. It must be noted that in the case of the pronouns in examples (e) to (h), *mashi* combines with the pronoun irrespective of the gender of the referent, and does not play a role in implying anything about the gender behaviour or identity of the given referent.

*Professionals*

Optional *mashi* also combines with nouns that refer to people occupied in different professions. Whether that professional is a woman, a man or a person whose gender is unknown, the results remained the same across the board. Examples include:

**Table 5.8 *Optional mashi 3***

| 12 Compound | Analysis | Meaning |
|---|---|---|
| (a) ɖakt̪ar maʃi | noun {doctor} + mashi | doctor (+ANIM) |
| (b) ɖiŋor maʃi | noun {police} + mashi | police (+ANIM) |
| (c) mist̪iri maʃi | noun {construction worker} + mashi | construction worker (+ANIM) |
| (d) d̪okand̪ar maʃi | noun {shopkeeper} + mashi | shopkeeper (+ANIM) |
| (e) bʰikiri maʃi | noun {beggar} + mashi | beggar (+ANIM) |
| (f) nərs maʃi | noun {nurse} + mashi | nurse (+ANIM) |
| (g) !minist̪ər maʃi/ ?mont̪ri maʃi | noun {minister} + mashi | minister (+ANIM) |
| (h) !ʈicar maʃi | noun {teacher} + mashi | Teacher (+ANIM) |

*Note*: '!' indicates constructions that sound odd or mildly unacceptable to the speakers; '?' indicates constructions that the speakers deem highly unacceptable.

As we can see, optional *mashi* combines with the names of professionals in 12(a–f) effortlessly, irrespective of source language. When it comes to (g) and (h) though, speakers have said that while it is theoretically possible for *mashi* to combine with these nouns, it sounds odd to them as they are not consructions commonly used by them. Further conversation revealed that hijras and kotis are frequently forced to drop out of schools due to their gender identity or effiminate mannerisms, and so teachers are not a regular feature in their lives by the time they join the community and start speaking Ulti. Hence the phrase 'teacher *mashi'* is barely used, if at all. Similarly, ministers are not figures most hijras and kotis have much access to, so conversations about them are not common in the community either.[1]

If we take the points raised above as valid reasons for why having *mashi* combine with 'teacher' and 'minister' does not sound quite grammatical to speakers of Ulti, then we can propose the following condition as a factor that governs which nouns *mashi* may or may not combine with: community access condition – where the combination of optional *mashi* with a noun is restricted by the lack of the community's contextual access to, and familiarity with, the given noun.

This condition is an extralinguistic, contextual factor that blocks the formation of certain *mashi* compounds. Since the blocking is not caused by any grammatical factors, it is highly possible that these compounds may be considered grammatical in a different sociopolitical environment in a few years' time, when the usage of these compounds become as common in the community as other compounds are.

### *Proper Nouns*

When optional *mashi* combines with proper nouns, it automatically gives it a kinship reading (13a–b). In other words, the *mashi* that combines with proper nouns is always kinship *mashi*, never obligatory or optional *mashi*. This can be verified by the fact that in 13(b), *mashi* does not combine with a proper noun whose natural gender is masculine, similar to kinship *mashi* as demonstrated in 5(b). Optional *mashi,* on the other hand, often combines with masculine natural gender nouns, as listed in 10(n) and 12 (this topic has been further elaborated below). Thus we can say that only kinship *mashi* can be used as an address or reference term; obligatory and optional *mashi* can never combine with a proper noun, therefore are never in a position to be used as address or reference terms.

**Table 5.9** ***Optional mashi 4***

| 13 | Compound | Analysis | Meaning |
|---|---|---|---|
| (a) | ninɑ mɑʃi | noun {Nina_F} + mashi | Nina(F) aunty (+ANIM) |
| (b) | *ʃurɟo mɑʃi | *noun {Surjo_M} + mashi | *Surjo(M) aunty (+ANIM) |
| (c) | ʃurɟo [ɖɑkt̪ɑr mɑʃi] | noun {Surjo_M} [noun {doctor} + mashi] | Dr. Surjo (M) (+ANIM) |
| (d) | ninɑ [ɖɑkt̪ɑr mɑʃi] | noun {Nina_F} [noun {doctor} + mashi] | Dr. Nina (F) (+ANIM) |

Curiously, when these same proper nouns are followed by the name of a profession, *mashi* can easily combine with them, as it now seems to be combining with the name of the profession rather than the name of the individual (13c). This means that *mashi* here is acting as optional, not kinship *mashi*, thereby enabling the phrase *ɖakt̪ar maʃi* ('doctor') to combine with the proper name Surjo, which the kinship *mashi* could not combine with directly.

*Nouns Ending in -ala/-ali*

When optional *mashi* combines with nouns ending with the suffix *-ala*/*-ali*, the judgement of the speakers regarding the grammaticality of the construction seems to be divided along gender lines. Speakers of Ulti find it ungrammatical when optional *mashi* combines with nouns with referents that have masculine natural gender (*-ala*), but grammatical when it combines with nouns with referents that have feminine natural gender (*-ali*). Examples include:

**Table 5.10** ***Optional mashi 5***

| 14 | Compound | Analysis | Meaning |
|---|---|---|---|
| (a) | *rikʃɑ-ɑlɑ mɑʃi | *noun {rickshawpuller_M} + mashi | *the rickshawpuller (m) (+ANIM) |
| (b) | rikʃɑ-ɑli mɑʃi | noun {rickshawpuller_F} + mashi | the rickshawpuller (f) (+ANIM) |
| (c) | *d̪ud̪ʰ-ɑlɑ mɑʃi | *noun {milkman_M} + mashi | *the milkman (m) (+ANIM) |
| (d) | d̪ud̪ʰɑli mɑʃi | noun {milkmaid_F} + mashi | the milkmaid (f) (+ANIM) |
| (e) | *mɑcʰ-ɑlɑ mɑʃi | *noun {fishmonger_M} + mashi | *the fishmonger (m) (+ANIM) |
| (f) | mɑcʰ-ɑlɑ mɑʃi | noun {fishmonger_F} + mashi | the fishmonger (f) (+ANIM) |

However, further discussion revealed that 14(b), 14(d) and 14(f) seemed grammatical to the speakers only because the *mashi*s there gave the phrases a kinship reading. As mentioned earlier, kinship *mashi* in Bangla can also be used to address or refer to older women not related to the speaker by blood – especially working class women. Data set 14 confirms that the same usage is acceptable in Ulti too. Thus, it can also be concluded that optional *mashi* does not combine with any noun ending in *-ala*/*-ali* to give a grammatical construction.

*Phrasal Nouns*

While most of the nouns that *mashi* combines with are bare nouns, there is one exception where optional *mashi* attaches with a phrase, as demonstrated in 15(a).

15 (a) [ɪsni pɔn] mɑʃi-t̪e
this side mashi.Loc
'On this side.'

This phrase, which usually appears without the *mashi*, can also appear as follows:

(b)! [ɪnsi] mɑʃi pɔn-e
this mashi side.Loc
'On this side.'

However, 15(b) is accepted as less grammatical, though not completely wrong, by speakers of Ulti. The most commonly used form of this phrase is

(c) ɪnsi pɔn-e
this side.Loc
'On this side.'

These three phrases all carry the same meaning; the presence of *mashi* does nothing to change its semantics. This brings us to the question: What does optional *mashi* do? Is it a term of endearment, perhaps an indicator of familiarity? Much inquiry probing into the subject revealed that it is neither; *mashi* can be used to refer to things one has no affection for, and to nouns one has not used before in a sentence, or in a given context. Hence, to properly understand the nature of optional *mashi* and what it does in Ulti, we need to look at how it behaves in an Ulti sentence.

### *At the Level of Sentence*

An analysis of sentential data in Ulti reveals that the presence of *mashi* affects neither the meaning of the constituent it attaches to nor its behaviour in a sentence. In the following examples, we see that *mashi* (in bold) can optionally combine with a noun in any position in a sentence – subject (16a), direct object (16b), indirect object (16c), adjunct (16d) – or in a VP (16e).

16 (a)

| [ʊnsi | rɑgi | ɖiŋor (**mɑʃi**)] | [həmsi-ke] | ɖɑk-cʰ-e |
|---|---|---|---|---|
| that | angry | police.3PS | 1PS.Dat | call.Pres.3P |

‘That angry police officer is calling me.’

(b)

| [həmsi-rɑ] | [ʊnsi-r | corki (**mɑʃi**)-ʈɑ-ke] | bilɑ | kor-e-cʰ-i |
|---|---|---|---|---|
| 1P.PlCla | 3PS.Gen | car.Cla.Dat | damage | do.Pft.Pres.1P |

‘We have damaged their(sg.) car.’

(c)

| [cipɑ] | [ʈunni (**mɑʃi**)-ʈɑ-ke] | [ʃɑt̪rɑ] | cɑm-i-e-cʰ-e |
|---|---|---|---|
| cipa.3PS | girl.Cla.Dat | clothes | take.Caus.Pft.Pres.3P |

‘Chipa gave the girl clothes.’

(d)

| [rɑm] | [d̪ol (**mɑʃi**)-t̪e] | [bou-ke] | [bʰiʃɑnt̪i] | ʈɑk-i-e-cʰ-e |
|---|---|---|---|---|
| ram | holi.Loc | wife.Dat | fish | eat.Caus.Pft.Pres.3P |

‘Ram fed his wife fish on Holi.’

(e)

| [ʊnsi] | [həmsi-ke] | [ɔnek kʰuʈni] | kʰuʈunsi (**mɑʃi**) | kɔr-e/kʰoʈ-e |
|---|---|---|---|---|
| 3PS | 1PS.Dat | many talk | talk | do.Hab.3P/tell.Hab.3P |

‘They(sg.) tell me a lot of things. ’

Furthermore, *mashi*’s occurence is not licenced by the transitivity of the verb (16b, c, f), nor is it dependent on the structure (simplex or complex) or source language (Bangla or Ulti) of the verb phrase (16f–i). In 16(b) the verb is transitive, while in 16(c) it is ditransitive and in 16(f), intransitive.

(f)

| ʊnsi (**mɑʃi**) | pɔt̪-onsi |
|---|---|
| 3PS | leave |

‘They (sg.) are leaving.’

(g)

| ʊnsi (**mɑʃi**) | pot̪-cʰ-e |
|---|---|
| 3PS | leave.Prog.Pres.3P |

‘They (sg.) are leaving.’

(h)

| ʊnsi (**mɑʃi**) | pɔt̪-onsi | kor-cʰ-e |
|---|---|---|
| 3PS | leave | do.Prog.Pres.3P |

’They (sg.) are leaving.’

(i)

| ʊnsi (**mɑʃi**) | ɟɑ-c-cʰ-e |
|---|---|
| 3PS | go.Prog.Pres.3P |

‘They (sg.) are leaving.’

The presence of *mashi* also does not have any effect on the agreement patterns displayed by the language. In 16(j) we see the verb agreeing with the subject for person, while in 16(k) we see that no object agreement takes place in Ulti, both irrespective of the presence of *mashi* in the sentence.

(j) ami/t̪umi/o **(maʃi)** d̪ɔrma ʈak-cʰ-i/-o/-e
1PS/2PS/3PS rice eat.Pres.1P/2P/3P
'I/You/They(sg.) (be) eating rice.'

(k) mali hʊmsi/t̪ʊmsi/ʊnsi **(maʃi)**-ke ʈanɖi ɟʰiri-e-cʰ-e
gardener.3P 1PS/2PS/3PS.Dat beat give.Pft.Pres.3P
'The gardener has beaten me/you/them(sg.) up.'

*Mashi* can optionally occur in almost all of these NPs, but there seems to be an aesthetic constraint against having two *mashi*s in one clause, no matter their distance. It is not morphosyntactically impossible to have them co-occur, but the speakers find the phonological realization unflattering and insist on using one *mashi* at a time in a clause or sentence. It is easier to have two *mashi*s when each of them occurs in different clauses, as seen in 16(l).

(l) həmsi-r piʈ **(maʃi)** bol-l-o ɟe kalke aɽijal bundi **(maʃi)**
1PS.Gen sibling tell.Pst.3P RP yesterday much rain

gir-e-cʰ-e
fall.Pft.Pres.3P
'My sibling said that it rained a lot yesterday.'

Thus we see that the occurrence of optional *mashi* in Ulti is not the result of any syntactic process. Further, it neither triggers nor blocks any syntactic process; its presence or absence makes absolutely no difference to how a sentence is computed in the syntax, or what denotation and connotation the noun it combines with carries. In other words, optional *mashi* is invisible in the syntax, and its occurrence in a sentence is purely a function of speaker choice.

## *Kinship vs Obligatory and Optional Mashi*

From the discussion above, we can also see that obligatory and optional *mashi* are different from kinship *mashi* in one significant respect. While the former can combine with inanimate (*khol mashi* – 'house'), abstract (*baebsha mashi* – 'business') and collective (*jojman mashi* – 'clients') nouns, the latter combines only with proper nouns and common nouns that have feminine natural gender. The nouns that obligatory and optional *mashi* combine with mostly carry a feminine or neuter natural gender feature (*mashi* combines with nouns with masculine natural gender feature as well but there is no speaker consensus on the matter, hence we will set these aside as special cases for now). Hence, one can theorize that the semantic gender feature that values for [feminine] in kinship *mashi* undergoes a semantic extension in obligatory and optional *mashi*, thus enabling it to combine with a much larger range of nouns.

One of the puzzles I faced while analysing the data was how to determine the exact value of the semantic gender feature carried by obligatory and optional *mashi*, given that the data present us with no conclusive evidence on the matter. This puzzle found its solution in the words of one of the primary participants in my research, Hema, who explained that since the hijra-koti community is mostly populated by trans-feminine/-femme persons whose deepest desire is to be accepted by the mainstream cisnormative society as women, they use *mashi* as a linguistic tool to fashion their identities and resignify the world around them as feminine.

Optional *mashi* in particular is therefore so exciting because speakers of Ulti actively insert it in the language by combining it with a noun in any position in a sentence – just because they can – in order to assert their gender identity in a larger society that has consistently denied them the power to do that, both sociopolitically and linguistically. Its usage, therefore, is a stylistic choice made by the speakers that also indexes their community membership, and becomes the vehicle through which they forge bonds of companionship, support and solidarity within the community.

Thus we can conclude that obligatory and optional *mashi* also have a semantic gender feature that values for [feminine], though, as discussed above, the range of nouns it combines with is much wider than that of kinship *mashi*.

## *Special Cases*

Optional *mashi* also combines with a series of nouns which have masculine natural gender, though there is a lack of speaker consensus as to the grammaticality of such constructions. Examples include:

**Table 5.11** ***Special cases 1***

| 17 | Ulti | Bangla |
|---|---|---|
| | (a) !parik maʃi – cishet lover | (e) *bon̪ʱu maʃi – friend(M)/lover |
| | (b) !ʈonna maʃi – cis man | (f) *puruʃ maʃi – cis man |
| | (c) !suɖɖʱa maʃi – father/old man | (g) *baba maʃi – father |
| | (d) !ʈæpka maʃi – boy | (h) *cʰele maʃi – boy |

It should be noted here that while many speakers of Ulti find 17(a–d) grammatical, many others find them completely ungrammatical. For the second group, *mashi* cannot combine with any masculine human nouns. Meanwhile the first group insists that this usage is fairly common in the Ulti speech community.

It would seem that while the judgement of the second group is completely in tandem with the analysis made above, that *mashi* carries a semantic gender feature valued for feminine, one could argue that the judgement of the first group – contrary to expectations – does not render that analysis false. Queer language has been known to often subvert gender expectations in different languages. For instance, in English, the words 'queen' and 'bitch', as well as the pronoun 'she' (in a process called *she*-ing), are commonly used by gay men to refer to each other, and in some cases, even to heterosexual men. The nouns or pronouns used in these cases are chosen to subvert the linguistic and social expectations that the gender value of a noun must match the natural gender of its referent.

I argue that a similar phenomenon is at play in Ulti when *mashi* combines with a noun with masculine natural gender. The semantic gender feature of *mashi* (feminine) does not need to match the natural gender feature (masculine) of the N1 (for speakers whose grammar requires this matching to happen, 17a–d are ungrammatical), and it implies nothing different about the gender identity or gender behaviour of the person who, for instance, is being referred to as a '*parik mashi*' instead of a '*parik*'. In other words, in this case, *mashi* is not literally gendering its referent, it is merely indexing, symbolically, the hijra-koti identity or the community membership of the speaker while subverting the expectation that the gender feature of the compound noun must match that of its referent if it has to be considered a grammatical construction.

Another point of note in this data set is that while *mashi* seems to easily combine with Ulti lexical items (wherever it is deemed grammatical), it gets blocked when it tries to combine with the corresponding set of Bangla lexical items. While it is well-established that *mashi* can combine with nouns irrespective of their source language, it seems that when a word in Bangla has a corresponding form in Ulti, *mashi* prefers to combine with the Ulti lexical item rather than the Bangla one.

In the following example set, we see that in the case of pronouns and demonstratives (18a–d), as well as human nouns and kinship terms (18e–h), the combination of Bangla N1s with *mashi* gives us completely ungrammatical compounds when there is a corresponding Ulti N1 that *mashi* can combine with.

**Table 5.12** *Special cases 2*

| 18 | Ulti | Bangla |
|---|---|---|
| (a) | həmsi mɑʃi – 1PS | *ɑmi mɑʃi – 1PS |
| (b) | t̪ʊmsi mɑʃi – 2PS | *t̪umi mɑʃi – 2PS |
| (c) | ɪnsi mɑʃi (Pro/Dem) – 3PS/This | *e mɑʃi/*ekʰɑne mɑʃi – 3PS/This |
| (d) | ʊnsi mɑʃi (Pro/Dem) – 3PS/That | *o mɑʃi/*okʰɑne mɑʃi – 3PS/That |
| (e) | ʈonnɑ mɑʃi – cis man | *puruʃ mɑʃi – cis man |
| (f) | lɑhɑrɑn mɑʃi – cis woman | *meje/mohilɑ mɑʃi – cis woman |
| (g) | suɖɖʰɑ mɑʃi – father/old man | *buɽo mɑʃi – old man |
| (h) | piʈ mɑʃi – sibling | *bon/bʰɑi mɑʃi – sibling |
| (i) | ʃɑt̪rɑ mɑʃi – clothes | !kapoɽ mɑʃi – clothes |
| (j) | d̪ɔrmɑ mɑʃi – rice | !bʰɑt̪ mɑʃi – rice |

However, in the case of non-human nouns, this merely plays out like a preference. That is, it is not ungrammatical to use a form like *kapoɽ maʃi* ('clothes'; Bangla N1) instead of *ʃat̪ra maʃi* ('clothes'; Ulti N1) in Ulti; it is just not a preferred usage (18i–j).

From the above examples, one may conclude that *mashi*'s first preference is to combine with an Ulti noun or pronoun or demonstrative. When such a lexical item is unavailable for *mashi* to combine with, it selects the corresponding Bangla, Hindi or English lexical item to combine with. Whether it is ungrammatical or simply not preferred for *mashi* to combine with a certain noun depends on the noun class it belongs to.

*Kinship Terms*

However, the story is not so simple when it comes to kinship terms. Besides the source language, another factor that governs the combination of *mashi* with a noun is the place of the noun vis-à-vis the hijra-koti social system. To elaborate, if a noun refers to a kinship term pertaining to the hijra *gharana* and hijra social hierarchy, *mashi* cannot combine with that noun. But if a noun refers to a biological kinship term or a relation that is commonly found in the cisgender community, *mashi* can combine with that noun (but only if it is an Ulti lexical item, as has been discussed above).

In the list below, the column on the left refers to identities commonly relating to transgenders, while the column on the right refers to identities commonly relating to cisgenders, which are clearly defined along binary-gendered lines. It must be noted that in all the examples listed on the right in example set 19, *mashi* is used as a reference term, not an address term.

**Table 5.13** ***Special cases 3***

| 19 | Hijra kinship terms | Biological kinship/mainstream relational terms |
|---|---|---|
| (a) | *gurumaʃi – guru | sʊɖɖʰi/sʊɖɖʰa maʃi – mother/father |
| (b) | *nanguru maʃi – guru of guru | ʈunni/laharan maʃi – cis woman |
| (c) | *cæla maʃi – disciple | ʈonna maʃi – cis man |
| (d) | *naek maʃi – area head/senior hijra | parik maʃi – cis male lover |
| (e) | *goʈ̤ija maʃi – co-sister under a guru | piʈ (laharan/ʈonna) maʃi – sibling (M/F) |
| (f) | *ɖ̤araɖ̤in maʃi – head of gurus | ʈæpka/ʈepki maʃi – son/daughter |

From this example set, we see that the set of hijra hierarchical and kinship terms form a semantic noun class in Ulti that functions exceptionally from the other types of nouns we have discussed thus far. The *mashi* compounding rule is semantically blocked from applying to this class, i.e. the nouns from this class cannot combine with *mashi* to form Ulti nominal compounds.

This is a curious phenomenon that does not fall in line with the analysis propounded above that *mashi* preferentially combines with Ulti and human nouns. The only way one could explain it would be to consider that the column on the left consists of lexical items exclusive to the hijra community and Ulti that have no separate counterparts in Bangla. Therefore, it would be redundant for *mashi* to combine with such identity-based terminology that is central to the conception of the hijra community, as *mashi*'s primary task is to create new lexical items for Ulti from existing words in various languages, and create a discursive universe that sets the hijra-koti subject at its centre and gives them the power and agency to describe – and gender – the world from their vantage point. The reason *mashi* can combine with the Ulti lexical items for biological kinship terms and heteronormative relationship terms is because they do not form the spine of the hijra social structure but are relationships common to the cisgender community, and therefore afford the scope to be 'Ulti-fied' further and made their own by the speech community.

## Conclusion

In this chapter, we analyse gender marking in Ulti through an analysis of *mashi* and its various types: kinship, obligatory and optional. The first marks kinship, the second creates new lexical items for the language, and the third acts as a symbolic gender marker optionally used by the speakers to index their community membership, perform and assert their target gender through language, and resignify the world around them in feminine terms.

However, the combination of optional *mashi* with a given noun or pronoun does not automatically imply that the referent is a feminine or femme figure. It merely is a linguistic tool intended to subvert the dominant, hegemonic, heteronormative and cisnormative discursive universe created by Bangla, which barely allows one any space or flexibility to perform and assert one's gender identity in terms not defined by a rigid, binary, heteropatriarchal framework. This subversion takes place through the use of Ulti itself, as well as through the use of optional *mashi* in Ulti, not just at a lexical and discursive level but also at a structural level. Optional *mashi* is not only used by hijra or koti speakers to resignify the world around them as feminine, but also to subvert the expectation that the combination of a masculine noun with a feminine gender marker must be ungrammatical, socially unacceptable or derogatory in any way for the man in question (for example, *parik mashi* – 'cis male lover').

The other thing that optional *mashi* teases out is a set of noun classes that combine with it in subtly different ways. The list includes sets of proper nouns, common nouns, pronouns and demonstratives, masculine natural gender nouns, human nouns, non-human nouns and kinship terms (Bangla vs Ulti; hijra vs mainstream relational terms). The factors that influence or block these combinations could vary from the source language of the noun, to the human vs non-human feature of the noun, to its grammatical category, to whether the noun has an Ulti form, and the contextual proximity and position of the noun vis-à-vis the daily lives and discursive universe of the average hijra and koti subject.

## Note

[1] Incidentally, in the city of Dhaka in Bangladesh, where a different variety of Ulti is spoken, the term 'politics *mashi*' is used to refer to a politician (anecdotal information).

# 6

# Encrypting Ulti

This chapter reflects on all that we have learned about Ulti thus far, and what that tell us about how well Ulti fits into and contributes to theories of code-switching, enregisterment and translanguaging. In the first section, we reflect on the status of Ulti and whether it should be characterized as a language, variety, code or register, based on what we know of the community and its relationship with Ulti until now. In the second section, we establish how Ulti can be described as a register based on the parameters suggested by Agha (2004). In the third section, we discuss the limitations of Agha's theory of enregisterment to characterize the processes that led to the formation of Ulti, in which the need to ensure that it remain secret played a fundamental role in the formation of its lexicon, structure and social function. We present the theory of encryption in this section to adequately describe the processes that underlie the formation of secret codes and registers such as Ulti. In the fourth section, we discuss how the multilingual environment in which Ulti operates can best be described through a representation of mental grammars in the human mind. We do this by considering the debate on translanguaging models between Otheguy, García and Reid (2015, 2018) and MacSwan (2017, 2020), where we conclude that MacSwan's (2017) integrated multilingual model of translanguaging is the best way to describe the aforementioned process.

## What Is a Language?

One of the fundamental questions that philosophers, linguists and scholars of various other persuasions have sought to answer for millennia is: What is a language? What makes something a language, and how do we identify one and distinguish it from other languages, dialects, varieties, registers, codes and so on? Can languages be thought of as discrete entities with sharp boundaries and no overlaps with one another, or do they exist in various linguistic continuums where they may share an indefinite amount of features with the languages they are in contact with? Who decides what a language is, anyway? The attempt to understand the nature and purpose of Ulti from a structural, sociopolitical and metalinguistic standpoint necessitates that we ask these questions once again, in the context of Ulti in particular and of hijra-koti languages in general.

One of the first things that we need to understand in this context is that a layperson's perception of what makes something a language is very different from a linguist's understanding of the same. A non-linguist would identify a language primarily through its lexemes and sometimes through its phonemes; a linguist, on the other hand, would offer a schematic representation of the various levels that combine and interact with each other to form a language: phonological, morphological, syntactic, semantic and pragmatic. While it seems obvious which conceptualization of language most would privilege over the other due to its academic value, it is also important to take into account the speech community's attitude towards and relationship with their language, since the sociopolitical and cultural dimensions of a language can often provide valuable insights into the lexical, grammatical and semantic composition of a language, as we see in the case of Ulti.

The speakers of Ulti have variously described it as a 'language', a 'code language' and an 'incomplete language', implying that the term 'language' is used loosely by them to refer to a linguistic variety that they recognize to have a limited repertoire of lexical items and restricted functionality as compared to the other named, majority languages they are exposed to, such as Bangla, Hindi and English. They recognize that Ulti is not *poripurno* ('complete'), not just in its lexical and functional range but also because of its reliance on Bangla content and system morphemes to construct a complete Ulti sentence. For them, Ulti is a secret code language – a mode of communication – that serves to obfuscate the contents of their speech so that they can avoid and avert the censure and harassment they would be subjected to if the general public recognized the taboo subjects of their conversations, which are mostly about hijra and koti lifestyles, professions and sexual relationships.

The secret status of Ulti is not just a product of caution on the part of the speakers, but also of the thrill they experience when they use it to mock and critique the subjects of their conversations in front of them, who do not realize and therefore cannot react to what is being said because they are not speakers of Ulti themselves. The ability to have this sort of camouflaged conversations in front of the mainstream public who have otherwise been instrumental in marginalizing and oppressing the hijra-koti community – the sense of power and agency it imbues its speakers with – is one of the main reasons why Ulti is so closely guarded and held so dear by the community.

Ulti, therefore, is significant to the community because of its social function: it is a marker of hijra-koti identity, a means of protecting themselves from harassment, and the means and site of forging lasting bonds of intimacy, companionship and solidarity within the community. It imbues its speakers with a sense of belonging with the community, and enriches them with a sense of self-worth and dignity that comes from knowing that one's selfhood and experiences are not shameful sociocultural or biological anomalies but valid human identities and experiences that many people can relate and speak to across time and space. The power of words in their ability to legitimize one's existence in their own eyes cannot be overestimated, nor their ability to forge a sense of community, solidarity and kinship amongst people who undergo similar experiences, especially if they are oppressive in nature. The language becomes a metaphor for the voice of the community; in finding Ulti, hijras and kotis find their voice as individuals as well as a collective, both within and outside community spaces. Therefore, we see that senior hijras who have a strong command over the language enjoy a position of considerable power, authority and influence in the community, and define the rules of the community and the standards by which community members must conduct themselves.

Thus, for the speakers, Ulti *is* the language of the hijra-koti community even if it is not extensive or ubiquitous enough to displace Bangla or any other language from their linguistic repertoire. There are many stakeholders who play various roles in determining what a language is and what it is not, from policymakers to linguists, but the most important stakeholder – whose opinion holds the most significance in this debate – is the speech community. When the speakers acknowledge a variety as their language, they take ownership of it, give it prestige within the community, and work towards maintaining it and passing it on to the following generations, which is what is happening with Ulti. Following the community, this researcher also continues to loosely refer to Ulti as a language even while trying to determine exactly how we can categorize Ulti from a theoretical perspective.

Ulti is especially significant for the community from a lexical standpoint. As mentioned in chapter 2, the dominant discourses around gender and sexuality that the community members have been socialized in since their childhood are conservative, cisnormative and heteropatriarchal discourses that characterize gender as a rigid, unchangeable binary category comprising only men and women. The languages these discourses are circulated in are standard Bangla – the dominant language – and its various regional varieties, as well as other languages that are spoken in the region. The silences around topics that are considered taboo and shameful in this discursive universe, such as non-conforming gender identities and sexual practices, are reflected in the lack of lexical items for these subjects in these languages (barring a few obscure, derogatory or archaic terms that are not used in regular conversations). Even though there are vibrant emerging discourses about non-conforming gender identities and sexual practices in a language like English, which is also spoken in the region, the discursive universe they circulate in is elite, upper-class, upper-caste, urban, and not accessible to most of the speakers of Ulti who exist at the intersections of their lower-class, lower-caste, and suburban/rural location(s). In addition, most speakers of Ulti receive their education in Bangla, which further alienates them from mainstream queer discourses that are almost always carried out in English. It is only in the very recent past that preliminary queer discourses have begun to circulate in languages like Bangla and Hindi, with queer characters gaining visibility and queer narratives – both fictional and real-life – finding voice and expression in media and popular culture. However, such emergent discourses are nascent and limited; the narratives they are built around depict only a small portion of the queer experience and are not representative of the wide range of subjectivities, experiences and perspectives that constitute the queer community. Among such narratives, too, the hijra-koti community remains poorly represented – both in quality and quantity. In such a scenario, Ulti continues to retain its significance within the community as it fills the linguistic and discursive gaps in Bangla through its range of lexical items that define, describe and articulate various aspects of the identities, experiences, relationships and lifestyles that make up the vast spectrum of the hijra-koti community.

In chapter 3, we see that the lexical items of Ulti are restricted to a limited number of domains that directly pertain to the social organization of the hijra subculture, their professions, bodies, aesthetics, customs and rituals, and so on. Anything that does not directly or indirectly relate to the life experiences of most hijras and kotis does not have a lexical item in Ulti, such as things related to music, education, agriculture, fishing, health care, law, etc. Some of the words may have corresponding lexical items in Bangla, but most – which encompass the range of taboo subjects in the language – do not. What this accomplishes, in essence, is that Ulti enables the community to express their own subjectivities and experiences, but not much else beyond that. The community dwells in a thriving multilingual ecosystem where each language in one's repertoire is spoken in various, often overlapping domains, and Ulti does not pose a threat to the status of any of them. Another reason for this is that Ulti is acquired later in life, when one starts interacting with the community; it is never acquired as a first or native language. In other words, it is impossible for someone to be monolingual in Ulti. Ulti merely serves to expand the discursive space and give voice to the subjectivities, experiences and lived realities of people who continue to be systematically denigrated, invisibilized and marginalized from mainstream spaces.

In chapter 1, we are introduced to the spectrum of secret languages spoken across the subcontinent by hijras and kotis. Their presence enlightens us to the fact that Ulti is not a unique phenomenon restricted to West Bengal; it exists in a vast linguistic continuum with these other secret languages that are spoken across the subcontinent – from Pakistan to India to Bangladesh. Linguists have variously described these languages as a 'lexical code' (Hall 2005), a 'code language' (Nagar 2008), a language (Khattak 2004; Khilji 2008) and a 'living language', as per Bell's seven criteria for determining whether a variety qualifies as a language (Awan and Sheeraz 2011b).

Even though these descriptions are ascribed to different varieties of these languages in different regions, there is a clear structural pattern underlying all of these varieties that allows us to treat them as comparable linguistic phenomena in their respective sociocultural contexts. Following Myers-Scotton's MLF model, it can be described thus: each of these secret 'languages' consists only of a set of lexical items that embed themselves into the grammatical framework of the matrix language, which in each case is the dominant language spoken in the region, i.e. Punjabi, Siraiki and Urdu in the case of various varieties of Farsi in Pakistan, Hindi in the case of the Farasi spoken in parts of north India, varieties of Bangla in the case of the varieties of Ulti spoken in West Bengal and Dhaka, and so on. Each of these varieties (as far as one can observe from available research) thus has some of the grammatical properties of the respective matrix languages, especially considering that these secret languages do not seem to have system morphemes or a grammatical framework of their own outside of the one from the matrix language they embed themselves in. In other words, the grammatical framework of Ulti and its counterparts look very similar to that of their matrix languages. This explains why some scholars have called them languages, while others call them lexical codes. While the former look at them as languages in their sociological and functional sense, and take their status as a 'mixed language' into account while describing them, the latter are interested in the potential of the lexical items unique to these languages to codify certain concepts, sociocultural practices and subjectivities specific to the speech community, and thereby define them as isolated linguistic phenomena that are divergent from the conventions and structures of their matrix language.

This prompts us to consider the question: Can Ulti be described in isolation or does it need to be defined in relation to Bangla? This question is fundamental in determining whether Ulti can be regarded as a language or as a variety of Bangla. However, we must also keep in mind that Ulti is not just a variety in relation to Bangla, but also in relation to the other hijra-koti languages from where it gets many of its words and word roots. It is the language of a social group – a sociolect – of gender and sexually non-conforming persons, just as Farsi and Farasi are. It can just as easily be regarded as a language in its own right with a lexicon and grammar of its own, regardless of how closely it might resemble any other language.

In doing so, though, we neglect the seminal role of the dominant languages in the creation of these languages: they provided the ideologically and culturally repressive environments that necessitated the development of such secret languages. Moreover, the centrality of the Bangla grammatical structure in Ulti cannot be denied, nor can the fact that Ulti needs system morphemes and many other content morphemes from Bangla in order to construct sentences and carry out conversations. Bangla provides Ulti with the stage to subvert its ideological certitudes and cultural conventions. Ulti is a marker of hijra-koti identity, but hijras and kotis have many other identities beyond their gender identity and sexual expression, and those are expressed, constructed and negotiated through Bangla and the other languages they speak in various domains and contexts. To overlook the significance of Bangla – which is predominantly spoken by most members of the community – and the other languages in the linguistic repertoire of Ulti speakers is tantamount to denying them their humanity by reducing them to their immediate identities and failing to acknowledge the complex, intersectional and multifaceted nature of their subjecthood. Ulti shares a broad intersectional space with Bangla, and therefore is best described in relation to Bangla from both a structural and a sociological point of view.

Chapter 4 looks at how Ulti is structured through the lens of Myers-Scotton's MLF model for bilingual code-switching. This model adequately explains the code-switching patterns between Bangla and Ulti content morphemes at the lexical level, and demonstrates how the grammatical framework of the resultant mixed language, Ulti, is almost identical to that of Bangla. However, in analysing Ulti through this model, it is important to acknowledge that we are not looking at how code-switching works between two languages, each of which possesses its own lexical items and distinct grammatical rules for combining them, but at one language and one set of lexical items that combine to form the mixed language Ulti. Here we see that the switch happens at the level of lexical items without effecting any change in the syntactic structure of the matrix language, indicating that the Bangla syntax perceives Ulti lexical items to be of the same kind – encoding the same set of features – as their Bangla counterparts.

In the process, we also see the formation of new lexical items (with the help of *mashi*), the presence of a few system morphemes (including the negation marker *nathi*, the relative pronoun *jinsi* and the question word *kinsi*) and one suffix (*-unsi*) in Ulti, which suggests that it is an expanding language which may be on the way to developing more content and system morphemes of its own in the next few years, if its domains of use and topics of conversation keep expanding comparably. We also see a few competing forms (in the verbal domain) and more than one surface realization for the same negation phrase (in the case of *nathi*), all of which encode almost the same meaning, indicating that the mixed language Ulti is in flux and could be developing syntactic structures and grammatical features of its own that diverge from those of Bangla in due course.

We also see, in chapter 5, the role of the symbolic gender marker *mashi* in coining new Ulti words as well as in symbolically indexing the feminine/femme gender identity and expression of its speakers by gendering the nouns it combines with. While it does nothing to block or trigger any syntactic process in Ulti, it is a central feature in the language that has developed as a direct consequence of the desire of the speakers to express their gender through their language. Languages like Farasi that have Hindi as their matrix language, and therefore have grammatical gender and participate in gender agreement, demonstrate a phenomenon of shifting gender agreement. The hijra and koti community is composed of persons assigned male gender at birth who have been socialized into using masculine gender agreement while talking about themselves. When these individuals take on a temporary feminine persona or permanently embrace their feminine gender identity, they switch their gender agreement to feminine so as to reflect their subjectivity through their language. When they subsequently take on a masculine persona or refer to themselves in the past when they socially lived as a man, they switch the agreement marker to masculine.

This practice of shifting markers of grammatical gender to align with one's social gender is a powerful move by the speakers of Farasi to exercise their agency and subvert traditional assumptions and discourses around gender by coopting the very language and linguistic conventions that were used to deny them their subjectivity and resignifying them on their own terms. This device is not available to speakers of Ulti because its matrix language, Bangla, lacks grammatical gender and therefore gender agreement. Hence, the speakers of Ulti developed the Bangla kinship term for aunt, *mashi*, into a linguistic device that performs a similar function as the shifting gender agreement marker does in Farasi: indexing the gender identity of its speakers through the language.

However, since *mashi* is not a feature in Bangla as it is in Ulti – it is semantically extended such that it can combine with a much wider range of nouns, including inanimate, masculine, directional and abstract, to form compound nouns – it is much more fluid and flexible in its role as a gender marker. It is not restricted to a rigid binary conception of gender; it can combine optionally with the range of nouns without implying that any of them are necessarily feminine or effeminate. Yet we analyse *mashi* as feminine because the speakers use it intentionally and productively in the language *because* it is considered a marker of feminine identity in Bangla. They use this form to reflect their own desire to identify and be recognized as feminine/femme, to gender themselves as well as the world around them as feminine.

Yet, speakers of Ulti occupy a wide spectrum of gender identities and expressions, some of which are fluid, ambiguous and complex in their multiplicity, and not restricted to narrow conceptions of femininity. While the language of Ulti is not extensive enough to lexically encode the range of these subjectivities and life experiences, the manner in which *mashi* is used does indicate that the speakers conceptualize femininity as a broad, overarching category that can encompass a range of persons, things, experiences and ideas – however conceptually odd or contradictory – within its fold. Ironically, the only class of nouns *mashi* cannot combine with are hijra identity and kinship terms, but its intentional and productive use in the language serves to normalize the idea that anything can be feminine – including persons who are born in 'masculine' or intersex bodies – and that expressions of femininity need not be restricted to specific expressions of one's bodily form, gestures, appearance, voice and other superficial markers of traditional femininity. The language has thus been harnessed to give voice to the concepts, identities and experiences that the speakers were kept from knowing, understanding and accepting since their childhood through the languages and discursive spaces they had access to. *Mashi*, therefore, can be considered a symbolic marker of the gender identity/identities of the speakers of Ulti, or, in other words, a linguistic marker of hijra-koti identity.

## Ulti as a Register of Bangla

Ulti, therefore, can be analysed to be a variety of Bangla spoken by a specific group of people, that varies from it in form and content to an extent that it is differentiable from the rest of the Bangla language. Another word for such a variety is a register, which has been described thus:

> A register exists as a bounded object only to a degree set by sociohistorical processes of enregisterment, processes by which the forms and values of a register become differentiable from the rest of the language (i.e., recognizable as distinct, linked to typifiable social personae or practices) for a given population of speakers. (Agha 2004: 37)

Registers are not stable, immutable linguistic forms; they can grow, decline or change as a result of the very kind of socio-historical processes that brought them into existence in the first place. Registers and their potential to change are predicated upon three sets of factors: the repertoire characteristics, range of pragmatic values and social domains of the register (Agha 2004).

The repertoire characteristics of a register take into account the repertoire size, grammatical range and semiotic range of the speakers. In the case of Ulti, we see that the speakers have at least two linguistic forms in their repertoire: standard (or any other variety of) Bangla and the corresponding variety of Ulti. It is somewhat grammatically distinct from Bangla as well, especially in the domain of verb phrase and negation (as analysed in chapter 4). The semiotic range of Ulti, which encompasses the 'types of linguistic and non-linguistic signs associated with the register's use', includes the set of lexical items unique to Ulti, and the gestures and type of claps that many scholars have analysed to be semiotic markers of hijra language.

The range of pragmatic values associated with a register includes stereotypes related to the user of the register, its usage, its setting of use, and positive or negative values associated with the register itself. As we have seen in the case of Ulti, it is almost exclusively spoken by the hijra-koti community, who have a wide range of stereotypes associated with their appearance, behaviour, professions, sexual proclivities, etc., both within and outside the community. Ulti is used both in safe intra-community spaces, and at the interface of the community and the outside world, to talk about subjects that pertain to the lives, experiences and desires of its speakers. The positive and negative values associated with Ulti can be broadly ascribed to the dichotomous attitudes that the broader transgender community has towards the language, where those who identify as hijras and kotis consider it a marker of their community and individual identity and regard it with warmth and pride, whereas the upper-class, English-speaking, privileged ones regard it with disdain for its local, vernacular associations and reject it to distance themselves from Ulti's less-privileged, lower-class, rural and suburban speakers.

The social domain of a register takes into account the existence of categories of persons that can recognize (at least some of) the register's forms, and categories of persons fully competent in the use of the register. Since Ulti is a secret language, the category of people outside the community who can recognize it is very limited, and restricted to certain friends, lovers and allies of the community members. However, there is a wide range of speakers who are fluent and fully competent in Ulti.

Thus we see that Ulti meets all the criteria to be characterized as a register of Bangla. It is a social as well as professional register that has cultural value and functions as a marker of hijra-koti identity. Besides that, it is also a distinctly expanding linguistic system that is gradually becoming structurally discrete from Bangla, thus giving us a glimpse of what seems to be the early stages of the development of the grammatical system of a new language.

## Encryption

However, the term register is not sufficiently adequate to characterize Ulti, whose defining feature is its status as a secret code. It is the secret nature of Ulti – and the speech community's desire to ensure it remains thus – that determines the fundamental social aspects of its use, including who speaks it, with whom, in which domains, for what purpose and to cover which topics. Registers are meant to function as in-group speech varieties, widely used within the social group it has emerged from and seldom outside it.

Ulti, however, deviates from such a pattern of usage. It is seldom used in closed in-group conversations unless the topic or the occasion requires it to be used. Formal announcements and conversations involving senior hijras are often conducted in Ulti, while more casual conversations that do not pertain to the domains in which Ulti is used – like sex, relationships and other topics related to the community – usually take place in Bangla or any other language the speakers may share amongst themselves. Ulti is not the lingua franca of the community despite being considered the language of the community. It is significant that the speakers, in fact, refer to Bangla and not Ulti as *amago khutni* (lit. 'our language'), indicating that being a hijra or koti is only one dimension of their identity, which exists alongside but does not overpower other aspects of their identity that come from their regional, ethno-religious, cultural, class and caste affiliations.

Ulti is most meaningfully used at the interface of mainstream and hijra-koti societies, where it serves to camouflage the conversation of the community members from outsiders and thereby protect them from censure, harassment and potential violence. In other words, it is in its role as a secret, encrypted register that Ulti is most valuable to its speech community. Registers are valuable for being markers of social group affiliation for their speakers, but such value is incidental to their existence. The secret status of Ulti is not incidental; it is intentional, motivated and carefully maintained so as to ensure that members of the hijra-koti community can survive and thrive with a certain degree of freedom of expression, safety and security in the hostile sociocultural environment they inhabit. Further, the need for a secret code to ensure the safety of the community gave rise to Ulti in the first place and influenced every aspect of it, from the choice of lexical items to its grammatical structure to its social role. The development of a unique feature like *mashi* can also be indirectly attributed to the secret status of Ulti, which created the discursive spaces necessary for the speakers to articulate their gender through language, in a way that was not available to them in mainstream physical or discursive spaces.

It is thus clear that the process of development of secret registers such as Ulti cannot be adequately described as enregisterment, as the term does not take into account the process of embedding, encoding and encrypting linguistic information so inherent and integral to the formation of secret registers. This process demands the coinage of a new term, *encryption*. Encryption can be defined as a sociohistorical process of development of a variety or register that is governed by the need to preserve its secrecy, such that the element of secrecy becomes one of the main reasons the variety or register carries linguistic and/or social value for its speech community. Encrypted varieties are maintained and intergenerationally transmitted in secrecy, but may not always remain a secret variety due to changes in the sociocultural environment that necessitated their secrecy in the first place. We see this in the case of the gay language Polari in Great Britain, which nearly died out once its gay and drag queen speakers gained social acceptance and political legitimacy in the country, and were not forced to live their lives in secrecy any longer (Baker 2019). Whether that will be the case with Ulti remains to be seen, but it will be interesting to observe how Ulti evolves if and when it will no longer be required to be a secret language for the community.

The other varieties of hijra-koti language, like Farasi, Farsi, Dhaka Ulti and any other unexplored variety, may also be characterized as encrypted varieties and registers after Ulti. However, one must be cautious not to use this term unilaterally to describe all hijra-koti languages; instead, one must examine each variety as individual linguistic phenomena taking place in their own specific sociocultural contexts, in order to expand one's understanding of encrypted registers and varieties, and add nuance, depth and dialectical layers to the theory of encryption.

## Translanguaging

Now that it has been established that Ulti is a secret register and a variety of Bangla, it brings to question the nature of code-switching at play in Ulti. When we analysed Ulti as a code-mixed language, we looked at Bangla and the lexical items of bare Ulti as discrete elements that come together to create Ulti sentences. But that is merely a convenient analytical device which does not capture the linguistic reality of Ulti and its usage in its entirety.

It has been mentioned before that Ulti thrives in a multilingual ecosystem and shares a broad intersective space with Bangla; what has been neglected in the code-switching analysis is the acknowledgement of Hindi and English as languages from which words and phrases are regularly borrowed into Ulti. We see evidence of their prevalence in the language from the way many new words in Ulti are coined by combining *mashi* with existing English and Hindi/Urdu words. However, most code-switching analyses, including the MLF model used here, take bilingual code-switching behaviour into account and isolate neat, idealized versions of the participating languages for analysis, instead of taking into account their behaviour as idiosyncratic combinations of various languages, varieties, styles and registers that blur into each other and make up a unique linguistic repertoire, or idiolect, for each individual speaker. Thus we see that such models are conceptually (if not analytically, at least in the case of Ulti) inadequate to characterize the kind of dynamic multilingual behaviour observed in the Ulti speech community. To describe that, we must turn to the integrated multilingual theory of translanguaging proposed by MacSwan (2017).

The concept of translanguaging was first described by Williams (1994), who was investigating teaching and learning techniques in a Welsh–English bilingual classroom in Bangor, North Wales. He, along with his colleagues, observed that students learn most effectively when they use all of the linguistic resources available to them in the classroom, which significantly includes their L1s (Welsh), whose use was not typically encouraged in their majority (English) language schools. Williams (1994) used the Welsh term *trawsieithu* to describe what Baker (2011: 288) characterized as 'the planned and systematic use of two languages inside the same lesson'; Baker later translated the Welsh term into English as *translanguaging*. The term soon gained popularity and has been used since to describe a wide range of bilingual and multilingual language phenomena, which in turn has led to very divergent ways of conceptualizing and theorizing the process of translanguaging.

One such theory of translanguaging stems from the following argument by Makoni and Pennycook (2007: 2), that '[l]anguages do not exist as real entities in the world and neither do they emerge from or represent real environments; they are, by contrast, the inventions of social, cultural and political movements'. In the words of MacSwan (2017: 168), 'These conclusions are motivated by a consideration of the colonial history of language names and their boundaries viewed through a postmodernist lens on language planning and policy.' The idea that there are no discrete languages leads, according to Makoni and Pennycook (2007: 22), to the dismantling of 'many of the treasured icons of liberal-linguistic thought . . . such as language rights, mother tongues, multilingualism, or code-switching'.

This position is endorsed by García and Otheguy (2014), García, Flores and Spotti (2017), Otheguy, García and Reid (2015, 2018) and Wei (2018), who concur with the argument that named languages are 'a social construct, not a mental or psychological one' (Otheguy, García and Reid 2015: 283). According to them, each individual possesses a unique idiolect or mental grammar which lacks any internal structural differentiation that might correspond to the grammars of socially named languages. García and colleagues call this the unitary view of language which precludes the possibility of the existence of bilingualism, multilingualism, and, consequently, the phenomena of borrowing and code-switching. It also 'rejects the idea that collections of individuals can usefully be described as linguistic communities; doing so, they argue, reinforces standard language ideology' (MacSwan 2020: 3).

Otheguy, García and colleagues seem to focus so closely on the impossibility of fixing rigid boundaries to demarcate the named languages (which they conflate with state languages) that they ignore the social reality that most named languages are not state languages, or the empirical reality that almost all languages or language varieties (including the unnamed ones) share linguistic resources with one another yet remain phonologically, lexically and grammatically distinguishable from one another. If bilingualism and multilingualism are constructs, then why is each person's idiolect different from another's? What is it that constitutes one's idiolect if internal grammars corresponding to named languages are not distinguishable from each other, yet are meant to be different for each speaker?

Further, they treat the concept of idiolects as stable and immutable, and do not explain what happens when an individual acquires a new language. If there is no differentiation between the internal structures of languages – which would imply that all languages share an overarching grammatical structure – then how do we account for the trouble learners face while acquiring or learning the grammatical rules of a new language? If all languages are socially constructed, are all grammatical differences socially constructed too? Even if all languages, like nation states, are constructed through social and political movements, why should that mean that they are not psychologically real for those who speak (or know of) them?

Language speakers have been able to distinguish between their language and that of others long before classrooms existed and taught students state-mandated, standardized varieties of languages. Speakers can distinguish between individual grammars and learn to switch from one to another even if they cannot always distinctly identify specific linguistic boundaries. Languages constitute speech communities who share at least one language amongst them and derive their sense of identity from the community. This social organization of linguistic groups is then harnessed to advocate for the rights and representation of that speech community on various sociopolitical issues. The social and political history and significance of such language movements cannot be erased in retrospect just by bringing into question the existence of languages itself, ignoring all empirical and theoretical evidence to the contrary.

The deconstructivist view proposed by García and Otheguy is based on their critique of language teaching practices which, they argue, have 'pernicious effects' because the instructors treat code-switching and bilingualism as exceptional and marked by presuming monolingualism to be the default. They treat the theoretical misconceptions held by the instructors that lead to flawed educational practices as flaws in the theory itself, which leads to the construction of a very myopic theory that does not take into account the social and psychological reality of how languages work in the world and in the human mind.

It is easy to debunk deconstructivism with the help of Ulti itself. All Ulti speakers do have an idiolect of their own, but each idiolect comprises a different set of languages, registers, varieties and styles that the speakers are capable of distinguishing by name or by their linguistic components, features and structures. We see that in the way Ulti speakers can switch from Ulti to Bangla and vice versa, which is a process they can recognize and identify because the participating languages and the act of switching between them is psychologically real and sociolinguistically meaningful for them. Moreover, the structure of Ulti and its varieties change based on the language or variety they mix with, which is further proof of the fact that each language or variety has a separate grammatical structure that might overlap with others but is not indistinguishable from them.

Ulti is also a marker of identity for the hijra-koti community; like every language, anybody can learn to speak it, but that does not automatically affiliate them with that speech community. It means something more for a speaker to identify and be accepted as a speaker of a language. In the case of Ulti, to be introduced to it and gain proficiency in it is a rite of passage for every new koti, that plays a central role in their journey of getting to know the community and forming lasting bonds of solidarity, familiarity and kinship with members of the community. Such practices of community formation mediated and forged through language are a key survival strategy for hijras and kotis in the hostile socioeconomic environment they inhabit, which is greatly cemented through the use of a shared language that is unique to – and gives voice to – the community, and imbues them with the sense of self-possession and confidence that comes with being able to articulate who they are.

The best way to theorize about the multilingual ecosystem that Ulti exists in, and the way it interacts with other (named or unnamed) languages and varieties, is with the help of the integrated multilingual theory of translanguaging. This theory, proposed by MacSwan (2017), takes bilingual processes such as code-switching, borrowing and translation into consideration to construct an underlying theory of translanguaging. MacSwan posits that:

> Bilinguals have a single system with many shared grammatical resources but with some internal language-specific differentiation as well . . . this perspective has emerged from codeswitching research, not the dual competence model, as García and colleagues assert. Extending the integrated view further, I will argue that multilingualism, not monolingualism, is universal, and that each of us, even so-called monolinguals, has multiple overlapping rule systems acquired through our participation in divergent speech communities. (Ibid.: 179)

This theory is predicated upon a fundamental distinction made between linguistic repertoire and mental grammar. A linguistic repertoire – or a social language (including dialects, registers, varieties or styles), as Gee (2014, 2016) calls it – has been defined as 'styles of using words, grammar, and discourse to enact a socially significant identity' in different social contexts (Gee 2016: 69). A mental grammar, on the other hand, is 'a set of interrelated components that are defined by the nature of the representations they generate and transform. . . . They are a small part of our overall knowledge of how to use language in social contexts, defining the narrow structural mapping from sound to meaning' (MacSwan 2017: 218). He further elaborates:

> A repertoire includes our richly diverse internalized mental grammars as well as the diverse vocabulary and systems of knowledge pertaining to discourse, pragmatics, and other social conventions that we recruit in verbal interactions with others. In Gumperz's (1964) terms, it reflects 'contextual and social differences in speech, subject both to grammatical and social restraints (pp. 137–138)'. (Ibid.: 188–89)

MacSwan represents the unitary and integrated multilingual models schematically thus, where G represents the mental grammar of each language, variety or register in the repertoire of a speaker:

**Figure 6.1** ***Models of mental grammars in translanguaging theory***

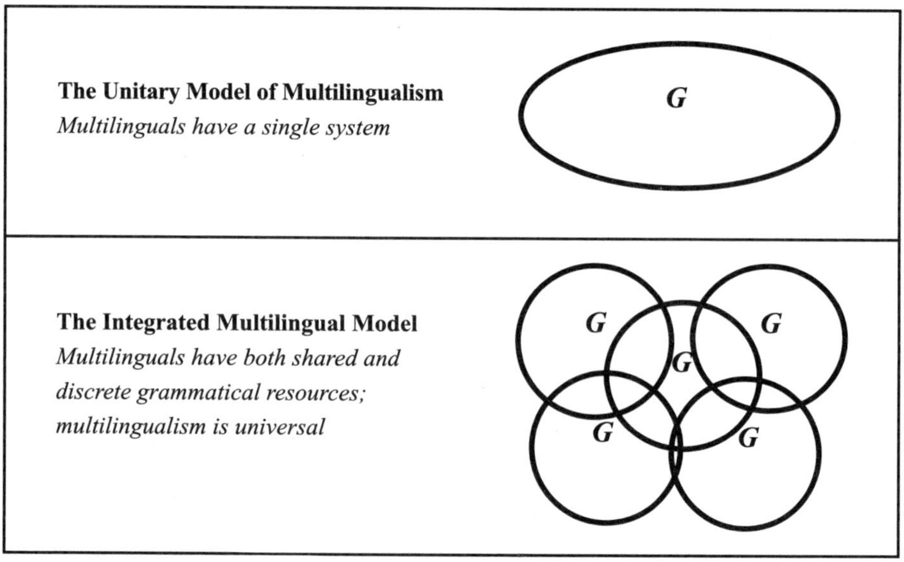


*Source*: MacSwan (2017: 180)

By MacSwan's model, we can characterize Bangla and Ulti as a language and a register, respectively, which share a lot of grammatical and lexical resources. They may also share some resources with Hindi, English and other regional varieties of Bangla, or with any other language or variety that may be part of a speaker's repertoire. This model undercuts the idea of a standard or fixed form of any language, but acknowledges that each speaker has a sufficiently discrete mental grammar of each language, variety or register in their repertoire which are distinctive enough from the others, and enable its speakers to communicate fluently with other speakers of that language, variety or register.

## Conclusion

MacSwan's (2017) theory of translanguaging takes into account the linguistic diversity and the possibility of many varieties of Ulti within a speech community, where each variety may have elements from more than two varieties, registers or languages participating in the formation of a specific style of code-mixed Ulti. Further, the study of such dynamic forms of language mixing and usage by this model does not depend on privileging one variety over the others in an attempt to fit traditional models of bilingual code-switching. Hence, MacSwan's integrated multilingual model of translanguaging is the best approach forward for future research, especially on multilingual communities which display unique and versatile patterns of language mixing whose analyses are ill-served by traditional models of studying bilingualism and code-switching.

Ulti also contributes an insight into a facet of multilingualism not hitherto addressed by anyone in the literature. As has been highlighted before, Ulti is not acquired by anybody as a first language; it is acquired by a process that is part learning and part acquisition. Apart from the lexical items unique to hijra languages, new Ulti speakers also learn to use new features like *mashi* in a new, motivated way that is different from the way they use it in Bangla, to index their community membership and gender identity. This indicates that translanguaging can be a deliberate and motivated process too, and not just an organic consequence of transnational immigration and the resultant multilingualism.

# Afterword

This book introduces the hitherto unexplored language of Ulti and tries to analyse and understand the social conditions and linguistic factors that have come together to enable the creation and sustained existence and growth of a language like Ulti. It also tries to understand the defining role that the gender identity, sexual behaviour, professions, culture and lifestyle of its speech community play in the formation, usage and internal structure – as well as the secret status – of Ulti. Finally, it examines in depth the relationship between linguistic gender and social gender, and analyses how the motivated manipulation of a language by its speakers to assert their (socially unacknowledged or rejected) gender identity can lead to the introduction of a new linguistic marker for gender in the language.

## Researching Ulti

The prospect of researching a secret language like Ulti presented many interesting challenges. The first of these was the prospect of analysing it linguistically without taking its social context into account, which proved to be a theoretically impoverished and practically untenable exercise. Ulti cannot be treated like any other language that linguists analyse by isolating linguistic data from their social contexts, because it is these very contexts that lend meaning to the lexicon, structures and functions of Ulti. Indeed, phenomena like *mashi,* which optionally and productively combine with so many classes of nouns, cannot be explained without understanding who is using this feature, around whom, and what its underlying significance is for the community.

As a corollary, it is equally impoverishing to conduct research on the languages used by hijra and koti communities without a deep lexical and structural analysis of these from a linguistic perspective, which provides powerful insights into the ideas and attitudes underlying language use by the community, and, by extension, into the lifestyles, social conventions and social organization of hijras and kotis themselves into an independent and thriving subculture. It also helps us distinguish Ulti from its regional counterparts in the way the gender feature manifests itself in the language, thus establishing that even linguistically, hijras and kotis do not constitute an undifferentiated homogenous mass across the subcontinent, but are deeply rooted in the culture, languages and customs of the regions they come from or have settled in despite sharing many common features and traits with each other across regions, religions and culture.

This gives rise to many interesting linguistic and interdisciplinary avenues down which Ulti research can be taken in the future, such as morpho-phonology, documentation, anthropology, queer feminist theory, culture studies and so on. Linguistically, one can document and analyse the lexicon and grammar of the hijra language spoken in a certain region, examine how it interacts with the mainstream languages existing alongside it, and, most crucially, analyse how the category of gender is marked and negotiated by the speakers of that linguistic variety. The wealth of data that can be mined from this part of the world and the variation and diversity they could display (as one can assume from the Farsi, Farasi and Ulti data we already have access to) would contribute to the development of a rich theory of transgender languages spoken in the subcontinent, which would subsequently be able to deepen our understanding of and insight into the variety of queer languages spoken across the globe.

Another challenge I faced when researching Ulti was due to the fact that these languages have been undocumented until very recently. Ulti, in particular, has never been linguistically documented before this, which makes it difficult to diachronically analyse it and see patterns of features emerging or disappearing from the language, and speculate on the reasons behind those changes. This book hopes to be the first step in remedying that, by presenting a lexical and grammatical analysis based on which the evolution of Ulti and the development of new, emerging system morphemes and other grammatical forms (like *-unsi* and *nathi*) in the language can be observed in the upcoming years. Such research can also observe if the level of encryption of Ulti gets tightened or more relaxed over the years, and whether that leads to a decrease or increase in the domains and spaces Ulti is used in, what kind of effect that has on the lexicon and grammatical structure of Ulti, and how that affects the attitude of the speech community towards the language.

The findings of this research not only add a nuanced perspective to theories of enregisterment, code-switching and translanguaging, but also present the concept of encryption, which describes the processes that govern the formation of secret registers like Ulti. It also has consequences for linguistic fieldwork techniques which need to develop nuanced ways of working in situations where the data to be collected are sensitive and secret in nature and the participants come from a socially vulnerable group. This research work demonstrates how motivated language use can lead to the development of a linguistic gender marker (*mashi*) that symbolically (but not grammatically) marks social gender on a language that hitherto carried minimal markers for morphological gender and none for grammatical gender. This process provides an insight into the complex and diverse ways in which femininity is conceptualized and encoded in the language, behaviour and practices of the hijra-koti community, which often do not coincide with one another, thus giving us a glimpse of the wide-ranging diversity and ambiguity that characterizes gender identity and expression in the hijra-koti community.

# Bibliography


## Acts

*A Collection of the Acts Passed by the Governor General of India in Council, 1871*, Governor General of India in Council, Calcutta: Government of British India, 1872, available at https://en.wikisource.org/wiki/Index:A_Collection_of_the_Acts_passed_by_the_Governor_General_of_India_in_Council,_1871.djvu, accessed 5 April 2019.

*Criminal Tribes Act (Act No. 27) of 1871*, 12 October 1871, retrieved from B&B Associates LLP, Advocates and Legal Consultants, https://bnblegal.com/bareact/criminal-tribes-act-1871/

Section 377: see https://en.wikipedia.org/wiki/Section_377, accessed 5 April 2019.

## Books and Articles

Abbi, Anvita (2001), *The Manual of Linguistic Fieldwork and Structures of Indian Languages*, Muenchen: LINCOM Europa.

—— (2013), 'Ancient Tribal Language Becomes Extinct as Last Speaker Dies', https://www.theguardian.com/world/2010/feb/04/ancient-language-extinct-speaker-dies, accessed 25 May 2023.

Agha, Asif (1999), 'Register', *Journal of Linguistic Anthropology*, vol. 9, nos 1–2, pp. 216–19.

—— (2003), 'The Social Life of Cultural Value', *Language and Communication*, vol. 23, no. 3, pp. 231–73.

—— (2004), 'Registers of Language', in Alessandro Duranti, ed., *A Companion to Linguistic Anthropology*, Malden: Blackwell Publishing, pp. 23–45.

Albarillo, Frans (2018), *Information Code-Switching: A Study of Language Preferences in Academic Libraries*, available at https://crl.acrl.org/index.php/crl/article/view/16765/18770, accessed 9 November 2018.

Alvarez-Cáccamo, Celso (1998), 'From "Switching Code" to "Code-switching": Towards a Reconceptualization of Communicative Codes', in Peter Auer, ed., *Code-Switching in Conversation: Language, Interaction, and Identity*, London: Routledge, pp. 29–48.

Anderson, Mary M. (1990), *Hidden Power: The Palace Eunuchs of Imperial China,* Buffalo, NY: Prometheus Books.

Arnold, David (1986), *Police Power and Colonial Rule, Madras, 1859–1947,* Delhi: Oxford University Press.

Aronoff, Mark and Kirsten Fudeman (2011), *What is Morphology?* second edition, Chichester, UK: Wiley-Blackwell.

Atkins, Beryl T. Sue (1992), 'Theoretical Lexicography and its Relation to Dictionary-Making', *Dictionaries: Journal of the Dictionary Society of North America*, no. 14, pp. 4–43.

Auer, Peter (1984a), *Bilingual Conversation*, Amsterdam: John Benjamins.

—— (1984b), 'On the Meaning of Conversational Code-Switching', in Peter Auer and Aldo Di Luzio, eds, *Interpretive Sociolinguistics: Migrants–Children–Migrant Children*, Tubingen: Gunter Narr Verlag, pp. 87–112.

—— (1995), 'The Pragmatics of Code-switching: A Sequential Approach', in Lesley Milroy and Pieter Muysken, eds, *One Speaker, Two Languages: Crossdisciplinary Perspectives on Code-switching*, Cambridge, UK: Cambridge University Press, pp. 115–35.

—— (1998), *Code-Switching in Conversation: Language, Interaction, and Identity*, London: Routledge.

—— (2021), '"Translanguaging" or "Doing Languages"? Multilingual Practices and the Notion of "Codes"', in Jeff MacSwan, ed., *Multilingual Perspectives on Translanguaging*, Series: Language, Education and Diversity, Multilingual Matters, pp. 126–53.

Awan, Muhammad Safeer and Muhammad Sheeraz (2011a), *Hijra Farsi Wordlist,* Islamabad.

—— (2011b), 'Queer but Language: A Sociolinguistic Study of Farsi', *International Journal of Humanities and Social Science*, vol. 1, no. 10, pp. 127–35.

Ayres, A.C. (1992), 'A Scandalous Breach of Public Decency: Defining the Decent – Indian Hijras in the Nineteenth and Twentieth Centuries', BA (Hons) thesis, Harvard University.

Ayalon, David (1999), *Eunuchs, Caliphs and Sultans: A Study in Power Relationships*, Jerusalem: Magnes Press, Hebrew University.

Bailey, Benjamin (2001), 'The Language of Multiple Identities among Dominican Americans', *Journal of Linguistic Anthropology*, vol. 10, no. 2, pp. 190–223.

—— (2002), *Language, Race, and Negotiation of Identity: A Study of Dominican Americans*, New York: LFB Scholarly Publishing.

Baker, Paul (2008), *Sexed Texts: Language, Gender and Sexuality,* London: Equinox Publishing.

—— (2019), *Fabulosa! The Story of Polari, Britain's Secret Gay Language*, London: Reaktion Books.

Balaji, Meena and Ruth Lor Malloy (1997), *Hijras: Who We Are*, Toronto: Think Asia.

Barker, George Carpenter (1947), 'Social Functions of Language in a Mexican-American Community', *Acta Americana*, vol. 5, pp. 185–202.

Benson, Erica J. (2001), 'The Neglected Early History of Codeswitching Research in the United States', *Language & Communication*, vol. 21, no. 1, pp. 23–36.

Bergenholtz, Henning and Rufus H. Gouws (2012), 'What is Lexicography?' *Lexicos*, vol. 22, no. 1, pp. 31–42.

Besnier, Niko (2003), 'Crossing Genders, Mixing Languages: The Linguistic Construction of Transgenderism in Tonga', in Janet Holmes and Miriam Meyerhoff, eds, *The Handbook of Language and Gender*, Malden: Blackwell Publishing, pp. 279–301.

Bhatia, Sakshi (2013), 'The Grammar of Code-switching: A Minimalist Perspective', MPhil thesis, University of Delhi, Delhi.

Bhimbai, K. (1901), 'Pavayas in Gujarat Population: Hindus', *Gazetteer of the Bombay Presidency*, Bombay: Government Central Press.

Blom, Jan-Petter and John J. Gumperz (1972), 'Social Meaning in Linguistic Structures: Code Switching in Northern Norway', in John J. Gumperz and Dell Hymes, eds, *Directions in Sociolinguistics: The Ethnography of Communication*, New York: Holt, Rinehart and Winston, pp. 407–34.

Bobb, D. and C. Patel (1982), 'Fear is the Key', *India Today*, 15 September, pp. 84–85.

Bock, Zannie (2011), 'Code-switching: An Appraisal Resource in TRC Testimonies', *Functions of Language*, vol. 18, no. 2, pp. 183–89.

Borba, Rodrigo and Ana Cristina Ostermann (2007), 'Do Bodies Matter?: Travestis' Embodiment of (Trans)Gender Identity Through the Manipulation of the Brazilian Portuguese Grammatical Gender System', *Gender and Language*, pp. 131–47.

Bourdieu, Pierre (1986), 'The Forms of Capital', in John G. Richardson, ed., *Handbook of Theory and Research for the Sociology of Education*, Westport, CT: Greenwood, pp. 241–58.

Breitborde, Lawrence B. (1983), 'Levels of Analysis in Sociolinguistic Explanation: Bilingual Code Switching, Social Relations, and Domain Theory', *International Journal of the Sociology of Language*, vol. 39, pp. 5–43.

Bucholtz, Mary (1999), 'You da Man: Narrating the Racial Other in the Production of White Masculinity', *Journal of Sociolinguistics*, vol. 3, no. 4, pp. 443–60.

Bucholtz, Mary and Kira Hall (2005), 'Identity and Interaction: A Sociocultural Linguistic Approach', *Discourse Studies*, vol. 7, nos 4 and 5.

Butler, Judith (1990), *Gender Trouble, Feminism and the Subversion of Identity*, New York: Routledge.

Campbell, Lyle (1994), 'Linguistic Reconstruction and Unwritten Languages', in Ronald E. Asher and James M. Y. Simpson, eds, *Encyclopedia of Language and Linguistics*, London: Pergamon Press, pp. 3475–80.

Carstairs, George M. (1956), 'Hinjra and Jiryan: Two Derivatives of Hindu Attitudes to Sexuality', *British Journal of Medical Psychology*, vol. 29, pp. 128–38.

Chatterjee, Indrani (1999), *Gender, Slavery and Law in Colonial India*, New Delhi: Oxford University Press.

Chomsky, Noam (1968), *Remarks on Nominalization*, Bloomington, Indiana: Linguistics Club, Indiana University.

Choudhury, Agnikaar (2015), 'Meet Dr Manabi Bandopadhyay, India's First Transgender College Principal', *Scroll.in*, 11 June, https://scroll.in/article/733484/meet-dr-manabi-bandopadhyay-indias-first-transgender-college-principal, accessed 6 February 2018.

Claiborne, William (1983), 'India's Eunuchs Have Fallen in Esteem', *Washington Post*, 7 April, p. 4.

Clements, K.C. (2018), 'What is Deadnaming?', *Healthline*, 18 September, available at https://www.healthline.com/health/transgender/deadnaming, accessed 4 September 2020.

Cohen, Lawrence (1995), 'The Pleasures of Castration: The Postoperative Status of Hijras, Jankhas, and Academics', in Paul R. Abramson and Steven D. Pinkerton, eds, *Sexual Nature, Sexual Culture*, Chicago and London: University of Chicago Press, pp. 276–304.

Connell, Bruce (1998), 'Lexicography, Linguistics, and Minority Languages', *Journal of the Anthropological Society of Oxford*, vol. 29, no. 3, pp. 231–42.

Corbett, Greville G. (1991), *Gender*, Cambridge: Cambridge University Press.

Crooke, William (1896), *The Tribes and Castes of the North-Western Provinces and Oudh*, Calcutta: Superintendent of Government Printing.

Das, Sumi (2020), 'Discrimination and Nepotism in the LGBTQIA Movement, West Bengal, India', online discussion over Zoom on Facebook, 2 August, available at https://m.facebook.com/story.php?story_fbid=10158474994657383&id=100004471295431&mibextid=Nif5oz&paipv=0&eav=Afam1Dzp-v8OUh8J8DbT3XVvmXNXvHMEjma03Rdd2i7gd5eCghKcNYJ14uupazQpNzE&_rdr.

Dasgupta, Probal (1986), 'Gerunds, Participles, and the Theory of Categories', *Bulletin of the Deccan College Post-Graduate and Research Institute*, vol. 45, pp. 7–18.

—— (2006), 'On Bangla Impersonals, Including Passives', *Bhashacintana*, vol. 1, pp. 2–17.

—— (2006–07), 'A Dependency Syntax of Bangla', *Indian Journal of Linguistics*, vols 25 and 26, pp. 15–97.

Dasgupta, Rohit (2013), 'Launda Dancers: The Dancing Boys of India', *Asian Affairs*, vol. 44, no. 3, pp. 442–48.

Doniger, Wendy (1999), *Splitting the Difference: Gender and Myth in Ancient Greece and India*, London and Chicago: University of London Press and University of Chicago Press.

—— (2003), 'Third Nature in the Kamasutra: The Asymmetry of Male and Female', Gender Studies Distinguished Faculty Lecture, University of Chicago, 21 May.

Dutta, Aniruddha (2012), 'An Epistemology of Collusion: Hijras, Kothis and the Historical (Dis)continuity of Gender/Sexual Identities in Eastern India', *Gender & History*, vol. 24, no. 3, November, pp. 825–49.

—— (2013), 'Globalizing Through the Vernacular: Gender/Sexual Transnationalism and the Making of Sexual Minorities in Eastern India', PhD thesis, University of Minnesota.

—— (2022), 'The Freedom to Dance: Performance and Impersonation in Lagan ("Launda Nach")', in Harshita Mruthinti Kamath and Pamela Lothspeich, eds, *Mimetic Desires: Impersonation and Guising across South Asia*, Honolulu: University of Hawai'i Press.

—— (forthcoming), *Globalizing through the Vernacular: Kothis, Hijras, and the Making of Queer and Trans Identities in India*, London: Bloomsbury Academic.

Ebden, Henry (1855), 'A Few Notes, with Reference to "the Eunuchs", to be Found in the Large Households of the State of Rajpootana', *Indian Annals of Medical* Science, vol. 3, pp. 520–25.

Enthoven, Reginald Edward (1922), *The Tribes and Castes of Bombay*, Madras: Asian Educational Services.

Epple, Carolyn (1998), 'Coming to Terms with Navajo Nádleehí: A Critique of Berdache, "Gay", "Alternate Gender" and "Two Spirit"', *American Ethnologist*, vol. 25, no. 2, pp. 267–90.

Ervin-Tripp, Susan (1964), 'An Analysis of the Interaction of Language, Topic and Listener', *American Anthropologist*, vol. 66, no. 6, part 2, pp. 86–102.

Fabb, Nigel (2001), 'Compounding', in Andrew Spencer and Arnold M. Zwicky, eds, *The Handbook of Morphology*, Oxford: Blackwell Publishing, pp. 66–83.

Faridi, F.L., ed. (1899), 'Hijdas', *Gazetteer of the Bombay Presidency*, vol. 9, part 2, Bombay: Government Central Press.

Ferguson, Charles (1959), 'Diglossia', *Word*, vol. 15, pp. 325–40.

Filliozat, Jean (1964), *The Classical Doctrine of Indian Medicine: Its Origins and Its Greek Parallels*, Delhi: Munshiram Manoharlal.

Fishman, Joshua A. (1967), 'Bilingualism With and Without Diglossia; Diglossia With and Without Bilingualism', *Journal of Social Issues*, vol. 23, no. 2, pp. 29–38.

—— (1972), *The Sociology of Language: An Interdisciplinary Social Science Approach to Language in Society*, Rowley, Mass.: Newbury House.

Freeman, James M. (1979), *Untouchable: An Indian Life History*, Stanford: Stanford University Press.

Gal, Susan (1995), 'Language, Gender, and Power: An Anthropological Review', in Kira Hall and Mary Bucholtz, eds, *Gender Articulated: Language and the Socially Constructed Self*, New York: Routledge, pp. 169–82.

García, Ofelia (2009), 'Education, Multilingualism and Translanguaging in the 21st Century', in Ajit K. Mohanty, Minati Panda, Robert Phillipson and Tove Skutnabb-Kangas, eds, *Multilingual Education for Social Justice: Globalizing the Local*, Delhi: Orient Blackswan, pp. 128–45.

García, Ofelia and Ricardo Otheguy (2014), 'Spanish and Hispanic Bilingualism', in Manel Lacorte, ed., *The Routledge Handbook of Hispanic Applied Linguistics*, New York: Routledge, pp. 639–58.

—— (2019), 'Plurilingualism and Translanguaging: Commonalities and Divergences', *International Journal of Bilingual Education and Bilingualism*, vol. 23, no. 1, pp. 17–35, doi: 10.1080/13670050.2019.1598932

García, Ofelia, Nelson Flores and Heather Homonoff Woodley (2015), 'Constructing In-between Spaces To "Do" Bilingualism: A Tale of Two High Schools in One City', in Jasone Cenoz and Durk Gorter, eds, *Multilingual Education: Between Language Learning and Translanguaging*, Cambridge, UK: Cambridge University Press, pp. 199–224.

Gaul, Neils (2002), 'Eunuchs in the Late Byzantine Empire, *c.* 1250–1400', in Shaun Tougher, ed., *Eunuchs: In Antiquity and Beyond*, London: Classical Press of Wales and Duckworth, pp. 199–219.

Gee, James Paul (2014), *An Introduction to Discourse Anaysis: Theory and Method*, fourth edition, London: Routledge.

—— (2016), 'The Vexed Nature of Language Learning and Teaching', in Rodney H. Jones and Jack C. Richards, eds, *Creativity in language Teaching: Perspectives from Research and Practice*, New York: Routledge, pp. 63–76.

Gliozzo, Alfio and Carlo Strapparava (2009), *Semantic Domains in Computational Linguistics*, Heidelberg: Springer Berlin.

Goldman, Robert P. (1993), 'Transsexualism, Gender, and Anxiety in Traditional India', *Journal of the American Oriental Society*, pp. 374–401.

Gordon, Steward N. (1985), 'Collective Crime and Authority in North India', in Anand A. Yang, ed., *Crime and Criminality in British India*, Tucson: University of Arizona Press, pp. 140–61.

Grosjean, Francois (1982), '*Life with Two Languages: An Introduction to Bilingualism*', Cambridge, Mass.: Harvard University Press.

Gudschinsky, Sarah C. (1956), 'The ABC's of Lexicostatistics (Glottochronology)', *Word*, vol. 12, pp. 175–210.

Gumperz, John J. (1958), 'Dialectal Differences and Social Stratification in a North Indian Village', *American Anthropologist*, vol. 60, no. 4, pp. 668–82.

—— (1961), 'Speech Variation and the Study of Indian Civilization', *American Anthropologist*, vol. 63, no. 5, pp. 976–88.

—— (1964a), 'Hindi–Punjabi Code-switching in Delhi', in Horace G. Lunt, ed., *Proceedings of the Ninth International Congress of Linguistics*, The Hague: Mouton, pp. 1115–24.

—— (1964b), 'Linguistic and Social Interaction in Two Communities', *American Anthropologist*, vol. 66, no. 6, part 2, pp. 137–53.

—— (1976), 'Papers on Language and Context', Working Paper no. 46, Language Behavior Research Laboratory, University of California, Berkeley.

—— (1982), *Discourse Strategies*, Cambridge, UK: Cambridge University Press.

Hall, Kira (1995), 'Hijra/Hijrin: Language and Gender Identity', PhD thesis, University of California, Berkeley.

—— (1997), '"Go Suck Your Husband's Sugarcane!" Hijras and the Use of Sexual Insult', in Anna Livia and Kira Hall, eds, *Queerly Phrased: Language, Gender, and Sexuality*, New York: Oxford University Press, pp. 430–60.

—— (2002), '"Unnatural" Gender in Hindi', in Marlis Hellinger and Hadumod Bußmann, eds, *Gender Across Languages: The Linguistic Representation of Women and Men*, vol. 2, John Benjamins, pp. 133–62,

—— (2005), 'Intertextual Sexuality: Parodies of Class, Identity, and Desire in Liminal Delhi', *Journal of Linguistic Anthropology*, vol. 15, no. 1, pp. 125–44.

—— (2013), '"It's a Hijra!" Queer Linguistics Revisited', *Discourse & Society*, vol. 24, no. 5, pp. 634–42.

Hall, Kira and Veronica O'Donovan (1996), 'Shifting Gender Positions Among Hindi-speaking Hijras', in J.B. Victoria Bergvall, ed., *Rethinking Language and Gender Research: Theory and Practice*, London: Longman, pp. 228–66.

Heller, Monica (1988a), *Codeswitching: Anthropological and Sociolinguistic Perspectives*, Berlin: Mouton de Gruyter.

—— (1988b), 'Strategic Ambiguity: Code-switching in the Management of Conflict', in Monica Heller, ed., *Code-switching: Anthropological and Sociolinguistic Perspectives*, Berlin: Mouton de Gruyter, pp. 77–96.

—— (1992), 'The Politics of Codeswitching and Language Choice', in Carol M. Eastman, ed., *Codeswitching*, Clevedon: Multilingual Matters, pp. 123–42.

—— (1995), 'Code-switching and the Politics of Language', in Lesley Milroy and Pieter Muysken, eds, *One Speaker, Two Languages: Cross-disciplinary Perspectives on Code-switching*, Cambridge, UK: Cambridge University Press, pp. 158–74.

—— (1999), *Linguistic Minorities and Modernity: A Sociolinguistic Ethnography*, London: Longman.

Herdt, Gilbert, ed. (1994), *Third Sex, Third Gender: Beyond Sexual Dimorphism in Culture and History*, Brooklyn, NY: Zone Books.

Herschfeld, Magnus (1935), *Women East and West: Impressions of a Sex Expert*, London: William Heinemann.

Hockett, Charles F. (1958), *A Course in Modern Linguistics*, New York: Macmillan.

Hopkins, Keith (1978), *Conquerors and Slaves*, New York: Cambridge University Press.

Hossain, Adnan (2012), 'Beyond Emasculation: Being Muslim and Becoming Hijra in South Asia', *Asian Studies Review*, vol. 36, no. 4, pp. 495–513.

Ibbetson, Denzil, Horace A. Rose and Edward MacLagan (1911), *A Glossary of the Tribes and Castes of the Punjab and North-West Frontier Province*, Lahore: Superintendent, Government Printing Press.

Jaffe, Alexandra (2000), 'Comic Performance and the Articulation of Hybrid Identity', *Pragmatics*, vol 10, no. 1, pp. 39–59.

Jaffrey, Zia (1996), *The Invisibles: A Tale of Eunuchs in India*, New York: Pantheon Books.

Janice L. Jake, Carol Myers-Scotton and Steven Gross (2002), 'Making a Minimalist Approach to Codeswitching Work: Adding the Matrix Language', *Bilingualism: Language and Cognition*, vol. 5, no. 1, pp. 69–91.

Johari, Aarefa (2014), 'Hijra, Kothi, Aravani: A Quick Guide to Transgender Terminology', *Scroll.in*, 17 April, https://scroll.in/article/662023/hijra-kothi-aravani-a-quick-guide-to-transgender-terminology, accessed 14 Januanry 2017.

Keymeulen, Jacques van (2010), 'Compiling a Dictionary of an Unwritten Language: A Non-Corpus-Based Approach', *Lexikos*, vol. 13, no. 1, pp. 183–205.

Khattak, S. (2004), 'Self Esteem of Hijra Community', Master's thesis, Quad-e-Azam University, Islamabad.

Khilji, Tahir (2008), 'The World of Zenanas', *In Plainspeak: Talking About Sexuality in South and Southeast Asia*, no. 3, pp. 12–17.

Kitts, Eustace John (1885), *Compendium of the Castes and Tribes Found in India*, Bombay: Education Society Press

Koeneman, Olaf and Hedde Zeijlstra (2017), *Introducing Syntax*, Cambridge, UK: Cambridge University Press.

Lahiri, Bornini (2011), *Case Marking of Asamiya in Comparison with Bangla for Animate and Inanimate Objects*, New Delhi: Parimal Publishers.

Lahiry, Suman (2008), *Koti Language*, Dhaka.

Lewandowski, Marcin (2010), 'Sociolects and Registers: A Contrastive Analysis of Two Kinds of Linguistic Variation', *Investigationes Linguisticae*, vol. 20, pp. 60–79.

Lewis, Gwyn, Bryn Jones and Colin Baker (2012), 'Translanguaging: Origins and Development from School to Street and Beyond', *Educational Research and Evaluation*, vol. 18, no. 7, pp. 641–54.

Lo, Adrienne (1999), 'Codeswitching, Speech Community Membership, and the Construction of Ethnic Identity', *Journal of Sociolinguistics*, vols 3 and 4, pp. 461–79.

MacSwan, Jeff (2005), 'Codeswitching and Generative Grammar: A Critique of the MLF Model and Some Remarks on "Modified Minimalism"', *Bilingualism: Language and Cognition*, vol. 8, no. 1, pp. 1–22.

—— (2017), 'A Multilingual Perspective on Translanguaging', *American Educational Research Journal*, vol. 54, no. 1, pp. 167–201.

—— (2020), 'Translanguaging, Language Ontology, and Civil Rights', *World Englishes*, vol. 39, no. 2, pp. 321–33.

Makoni, Sinfree and Alastair Pennycook (2007), 'Disinventing and Reconstituting Languages', in Sinfree Makoni and Alastair Pennycook, eds, *Disinventing and Reconstituting Languages*, Clevedon: Multilingual Matters, pp. 1–41.

Manucci, Niccolao (1907), *Storia do Mogor or Mogul India 1603–1708*, vol. 2, translated by William Irvine, London: J. Murray.

Marmon, Shaun (1995), *Eunuchs and Sacred Boundaries in Islamic Society*, New York: Oxford University Press.

McWhorter, John (2014), 'Why Save a Language?', *The New York Times*, 5 December, available at https://www.nytimes.com/2014/12/07/opinion/sunday/why-save-a-language.html, accessed 3 July 2020.

Menon, Nikitha (2019), 'Enhancing the Voice of the Khwaja-Sera Community: An Interview with "The Noble Half" Filmmaker Khaula Malik', *Brown Girl Magazine*, 3 September, available at https://browngirlmagazine.com/enhancing-the-voice-of-the-khwaja-sera-community-an-interview-with-the-noble-half-filmmaker-khaula-malik/, accessed 12 August 2020.

Michelraj, M. (2015), 'Historical Evolution of Transgender Community in India', *Asian Review of Social Sciences*, vol. 4, no. 1, pp. 17–19.

Milroy, Lesley and Pieter Muysken, eds (1995), *One Speaker, Two Languages: Crossdisciplinary Perspectives on Code-Switching*, Cambridge, UK: Cambridge University Press.

Mitamura, Taisuke (1970), *Chinese Eunuchs: The Structure of Intimate Politics*, China: C.E. Tuttle Company.

Mitra, Nirmal (1983), 'The Making of a "Hijra"', *Onlooker*, 18 February, pp. 14–25.

Moe, Ronald (2003), 'Compiling Dictionaries Using Semantic Domains', *Lexicos*, vol. 13, pp. 215–23.

Morcom, Anna (2013), *Illicit Worlds of Indian Dance: Cultures of Exclusion*, New York: Oxford University Press.

Mosel, Ulrike (n.d.), 'Dictionary Making in Endangered Speech Communities', University of Kiel, available at https://www.mpi.nl/world/lrec/2002/papers/lrec-pap-07-Dictionary_Endangered_SpComm.pdf, accessed 13 May 2017.

Myers-Scotton, Carol (1983a), 'Comment: Markedness and Code Choice', *International Journal of the Sociology of Language*, vol. 39, pp. 119–28.

—— (1983b), 'The Negotiation of Identities in Conversation: A Theory of Markedness and Code Choice', *International Journal of the Sociology of Language*, vol. 44, pp. 115–36.

—— (1993a), *Social Motivations for Codeswitching: Evidence from Africa*, Oxford: Clarendon Press.

—— (1993b), *Duelling Languages: Grammatical Structure in Codeswitching*, Oxford: Clarendon Press.

—— (1997), 'Code-Switching', in Florian Coulmas, ed., *The Handbook of Sociolinguistics*, Oxford and Cambridge, Mass.: Blackwell Publishing, pp. 217–37.

—— (2004), *How Codeswitching as an Available Option Empowers Bilinguals*, Essen: LAUD.

—— (2010), *Contact Linguistics: Bilingual Encounters and Grammatical Outcomes*, New York: Oxford University Press.

—— (2001a), 'Calculating Speakers: Codeswitching in a Rational Choice Model', *Language in Society*, vol. 30, pp. 1–28

—— (2001b), 'Four Types of Morpheme: Evidence from Aphasia, Code Switching, and Second-Language Acquisition', *Linguistics*, vol. 38, no. 6, pp. 1053–100.

Myers-Scotton, Carol and Janice L. Jake (2001), 'Explaining Aspects of Code-Switching and Their Implications', in Janet Nicol, ed., *One Mind, Two Languages: Bilingual Language Processing*, Oxford: Blackwell Publishing, pp. 84–116.

—— (2009), 'A Universal Model of Code-Switching and Bilingual Language Processing and Production', in Barbara E. Bullock and Almeida J. Toribio, eds, *The Cambridge Handbook of Linguistic Code-Switching*, Cambridge, UK: Cambridge University Press, pp. 336–57.

Nagar, Ila (2008), *Language, Gender and Identity: The Case of Kotis in Lucknow India*, Ohio: Ohio State University.

—— (2019), *Being Janana: Language and Sexuality in Contemporary India*, Abingdon, Oxon and New York: Routledge.

Naim, C.M. (1979), 'The Theme of Homosexual (Pederastic) Love in Pre-Modern Urdu Poetry', in Muhammad Umar Memon, ed., *Studies in the Urdu Ġazal and Prose Fiction*, Madison: University of Wisconsin, pp. 120–42.

NALDIC (National Association for Language Development in the Curriculum) (2016), 'What is Translanguaging?', *EAL Journal*, available at https://ealjournal.org/2016/07/26/what-is-translanguaging/#:~:text=Translanguaging%20is%20the%20act%20performed%20by%20bilinguals%20of,Translanguaging%20is%20about%20communication%2C%20not%20about%20language%20itself, accessed 16 February 2021.

Nanda, Serena (1990), *Neither Man nor Woman: The Hijras of India*, Belmont: Wadsworth Publishing Company.

—— (1994), 'Hijras: An Alternative Sex and Gender Role in India', in Gilbert Herdt, ed., *Third Sex/Third Gender*, New York: Zone Books, pp. 373–418.

—— (1999), *The Hijras of India: Neither Man nor Woman*, Belmont: Wadsworth Publishing Company.

Nigam, Sanjay (1990), 'Disciplining and Policing the "Criminals by Birth", Part 1: The Making of A Colonial Stereotype – The Criminal Tribes and Castes of North India', *Indian Economic and Social History Review*, vol. 27, no. 2, pp. 131–64.

Nilep, Chad (2006), '"Code Switching" in Sociocultural Linguistics', *Colorado Research in Linguistics*, vol. 19, doi: https://doi.org/10.25810/hnq4-jv62

Nishimura, Miwa (1992), 'Language Choice and In-Group Identity Among Canadian Niseis', *Journal of Asian Pacific Communication*, vol. 3, no. 1, pp. 97–113.

Norton, Rictor (2002), 'A Critique of Social Constructionism and Post-Modern Queer Theory', 16 July, available at http://rictornorton.co.uk/social23.htm, accessed 11 September 2016.

Opler, Morris E. (1960), 'The Hijara (Hermaphrodites) of India and Indian National Character: A Rejoinder', *American Anthropologist*, vol. 62, no. 3, pp. 505–11.

Otheguy, Ricardo, Ofelia García and Wallis Reid (2015), 'Clarifying Translanguaging and Deconstructing Named Languages: A Perspective from Linguistics', *Applied Linguistics Review*, vol. 6, no. 3, pp. 281–307.

—— (2018), 'A Translanguaging View of the Linguistic System of Bilinguals', *Applied Linguistics Review*, vol. 10, no. 4, pp. 1–27.

Paolillo, John C. (2011), '"Conversational" Codeswitching on Usenet and Internet Relay Chat', available at https://www.languageatinternet.org/articles/2011/Paolillo, accessed 23 July 2018.

Parida, Ananya (2018), 'Hijra (Hijaḍā)', in Jeffery D. Long, Rita D. Sherma, Pankaj Jain and Madhu Khanna, eds, *Hinduism and Tribal Religions*, Encyclopedia of Indian Religions, Dordrecht: Springer.

Pattanaik, Devdutt (2014), *Shikhandi and Other Queer Tales They Don't Tell You*, New Delhi: Penguin India and Zubaan.

Peirce, Leslie P. (1993), *The Imperial Harem: Women and Sovereignty in the Ottoman Empire*, New York: Oxford University Press.

Peletz, Michael G. (2009), *Gender Pluralism: Southeast Asia Since Early Modern Times*, London: Routledge.

Popova, Maria (2015), 'How Naming Confers Dignity Upon Life and Gives Meaning to Existence', 23 July, available at https://www.brainpickings.org/2015/07/23/robin-wall-kimmerer-gathering-moss-naming/, accessed 12 July 2020.

Preston, Laurence W. (1987), 'A Right to Exist: Eunuchs and the State in Nineteenth-Century', *Modern Asian Studies*, vol. 21, no. 2, pp. 371–87.

Pride, John B. (1979), 'A Transactional View of Speech Functions and Codeswitching', in William C. McCormack and Stephen A. Wurm, eds, *Language and Society: Anthropological Issues*, The Hague: Mouton, pp. 27–54.

Radhakrishna, Meena (1989), 'The Criminal Tribes Act in Madras Presidency: Implications for Itinerant Trading Communities', *Indian Economic and Social History Review*, vol. 26, no. 3, pp. 269–95.

Rahman, Anisur (1990), 'Some Recent English Translations of Modern Urdu Poetry', *Annual of Urdu Studies*, vol. 7, p. 117.

Rampton, Ben (1995), *Crossing: Language and Ethnicity among Adolescents*, London: Longman.

Reddy, Gayatri (2005), *With Respect to Sex: Negotiating Hijra Identity in South India*, Chicago, IL: University of Chicago Press.

Ringrose, Kathryn M. (2003), *The Perfect Servant: Eunuchs and the Social Construction of Gender in Byzantium*, Chicago, IL: University of Chicago Press.

Rose, Horace A. (1919), *A Glossary of the Tribes and Castes of the North-Western Frontier Provinces and the Protected Territories of the North Western Frontier Provinces*, vol. 2, Delhi: Amar Prakashan.

Russell, Robert Vane and Rai Bahadur Hira Lal (1916), *Tribes and Castes of the Central Provinces of India*, London: Macmillan & Co.

Rutter, Eldon (1928), 'The Haram of El Medina', in Eldon Rutter, *The Holy Cities of Arabia*, London: G.P. Putnam's Sons, pp. 225–40.

Sanghvi, Malavika (1984), 'Walking the Wild Side', *The Illustrated Weekly of India*, 11 March, pp. 25–28.

Seabrook, Jeremy (1999), *Love in a Different Climate: Men Who Have Sex with Men in India*, London: Verso.

Shah, Arvind (1961), 'A Note on the Hijras of Gujarat', *American Anthropologist*, vol. 63, no. 6, pp. 1325–30.

Shah, Mashal (2013), 'The Khwaja Seras: Pakistan's Endangered Minority', *Huffpost*, 13 August, available at https://www.huffpost.com/entry/pakistans-endangered-spec_b_3732591, accessed 24 September 2016.

Sharma, Satish Kumar (1989), *Hijras, the Labelled Deviants*, New Delhi: Gian Publishing House.

Shortt, John (1873), 'The Kojahs of Southern India', *The Journal of the Anthropological Institute of Great Britain and Ireland*, vol. 2, pp. 402–07.

Sideris, G. (2002), '"Eunuchs of Light": Power, Imperial Ceremonial and Positive Representations of Eunuchs in Byzantium (4th–12th Centuries)', in Shaun Tougher, ed., *Eunuchs: in Antiquity and Beyond*, London: Classical Press of Wales and Duckworth, pp. 161–76.

Sinha, A. (1967), ' Procreation Among the Eunuchs', *Eastern Anthropologist*, vol. 20, no. 2, pp. 168–76.

Snigdha, Rezwana Karim (2021), 'Beyond Binaries: An Ethnographic Study of Hijra in Dhaka, Bangladesh', PhD thesis, Auckland University of Technology, New Zealand.

Sorensen, Janet (2004), 'Vulgar Tongues: Canting Dictionaries and the Language of the People in Eighteenth-Century Britain', *Eighteenth-Century Studies*, vol. 37, no. 3, Spring, pp. 435–54.

Srivastava, Sanjay (2001), 'Introduction', in Sanjay Srivastava, ed., *Sexual Sites, Seminal Attitudes: Sexualities, Masculinities and Culture in South Asia*, pp. 1–24.

Storch, Anne (2011), *Secret Manipulations: Language and Context in Africa*, Oxford: Oxford University Press.

Swadesh, Morris (1955), 'Towards Greater Accuracy in Lexicostatistic Dating', *International Journal of American Linguistics*, vol. 21, no. 2, pp. 121–37.

Sweet, Michael J. and Leonard Zwilling (1993), 'The First Medicalization: The Taxonomy and Etiology of Queerness in Classical Indian Medicine', *Journal of the History of Sexuality*, vol. 3, no. 4, pp. 590–607.

Thurston, Edgar (1909), *Castes and Tribes of Southern India*, Madras: Government Press.

Tolen, Rachen J. (1991), 'Colonizing and Transforming the Criminal Tribesman: The Salvation Army in British India', *American Ethnologist*, vol. 18, no. 1, pp. 106–25.

Torras, Maria-Carme and Joseph Gafaranga (2002), 'Social Identities and Language Alternation in Non-Formal Institutional Bilingual Talk: Trilingual Service Encounters in Barcelona', *Language in Society*, vol. 31, no. 4, pp. 527–48.

Tougher, Shaun (2002), 'In or Out? Origins of Court Eunuchs', in S. Tougher, ed., *Eunuchs: In Antiquity and Beyond*, London: Classical Press of Wales and Duckworth, pp. 143–60.

Tsai, Shih-Shan Henry (1996), *The Eunuchs in the Ming Dynasty*, Albany: SUNY Press.

UK Essays (2018), 'The History and Principles of Lexicography', November, available at https://www.ukessays.com/essays/english-language/the-history-and-principles-of-lexicography-english-language-essay.php?vref=1, accessed 5 December 2019.

van den Berg, René and Susan Shore (2006), 'A New Mass Elicitation Technique: The Dictionary Development Program', paper presented at the Tenth International Conference on Austronesian Linguistics (10ICAL), Puerto Princesa City, Palawan, Philippines.

Vanita, Ruth and Saleem Kidwai (2000), *Same-Sex Love in India: Readings from Literature and History*, London: Palgrave Macmillan.

Vatsyayana (2002), *Kamasutra: A New, Complete English Translation of the Sanskrit Text: With Excerpts from the Sanskrit Jayamangala Commentary of Yashodhara Indrapada, the Hindi Jaya Commentary of Devadatta Shastri, and Explanatory Notes by the Translators*, with contributions from Wendy Doniger and Sudhir Kakar, New York: Oxford University Press.

Vogt, Hans (1954), 'Language Contacts', *Word*, vol. 10, nos 2 and 3, pp. 365–74.

Vyas, M.D. and Yogesh Shingala (1987), *The Life Style of the Eunuchs*, New Delhi: Anmol Publications.

Weedon, Chris (1997), *Feminist Practice and Post-Structuralist Theory*, second edition, Oxford: Blackwell.

Wei, Li (2018), 'Translanguaging as a Practical Theory of Language', *Applied Linguistics*, vol. 39. no. 1, pp. 9–30.

Wei, Li and Hua Zhu (2013), 'Translanguaging Identities and Ideologies: Creating Transnational Space Through Flexible Multilingual Practices Amongst Chinese University Students in the UK', *Applied Linguistics*, vol. 34, no. 5, pp. 516–35.

Weinreich, Uriel (1953), *Languages in Contact*, The Hague: Mouton.

Williams, Cen (1994), 'Afarniad o Ddulliau Dysgu ac Addysgu yng Nghyd-destun Addysg Uwchradd Ddwyieithog' (An Evaluation of Teaching and Learning Methods in the Context of Bilingual Secondary Education), Doctoral dissertation, University of Wales, Bangor.

Williams, Raymond (1977), 'Dominant, Residual and Emergent', in *Marxism and Literature*, Oxford and New York: Oxford University Press.

Yang, Anand A. (1985), *Crime and Criminality in British India*, Tucson: University of Arizona Press.

Zimman, Lal (2014), 'The Discursive Construction of Sex: Remaking and Reclaiming the Gendered Body in Talk about Genitals among Trans Men', in Lal Zimman, Jenny L. Davis and Joshua Raclaw, eds, *Queer Excursions: Retheorizing Binaries in Language, Gender, and Sexuality*, Oxford and New York: Oxford University Press, pp. 13–34.

Zimman, Lal and Kira Hall (2010), 'Language, Embodiment, and the "Third Sex"', in Dominic Watt and Carmen Llamas, *Language and Identities*, Edinburgh: Edinburgh University Press, pp. 166–78.

Zwilling, Leonard and Michael J. Sweet (1996), '"Like a City Ablaze": The Third Sex and the Creation of Sexuality in Jain Religious Literature', *Journal of the History of Sexuality*, vol. 6, no. 3, pp. 359–84.

Zysk, Kenneth G. (1991), *Asceticism and Healing in Ancient India: Medicine in the Buddhist Monastery*, Delhi: Motilal Banarsidass Publishers.

## INTERVIEWS

Collection of field notes and interviews with members of the hijra-koti community, 2017–2020, Kalyani, West Bengal.

Bony Das, 15 February 2020, Kalyani, West Bengal.

Aniruddha Dutta, 15 November 2020, Kalyani, West Bengal.